Planning *for* Community-Oriented Health Systems

James E. Rohrer

APHA

American Public Health Association

3M11/96

The Library of Congress has cataloged this work as follows:
American Public Health Association
        Planning for Community-Oriented Health Systems
Library of Congress Catalog Card Number: 96-078610

ISBN: 0-87553-230-6

Printed and bound in the United States of America.
  Book Design: Ellen T. Meyer, APHA
  Cover Design: Dever Designs, Laurel, Maryland
  Typesetting: Marilyn B. Butler, APHA
    Set in: Palatino
  Printing and Binding: United Book Press, Inc., Baltimore, Maryland

Acknowledgments

THE IDEAS PRESENTED IN THIS BOOK WERE SIGNIFICANTLY influenced by my collaboration with Dr James Merchant. Ultimately, my deep involvement with community health planning would have been unlikely without Dr Merchant's encouragement and support.

The ideas presented in these pages reflect recent experience with 10 community health planning projects. Some of these projects were handled by my students and led by community organizations; others were guided almost exclusively by me. Financial support was varied: some projects were funded by the Health Resources and Services Administration (as educational exercises), some by the Agency for Health Care Policy and Research (as demonstration project sites), some by the Health of the Public project, initiated by the Pew and Robert Wood Johnson foundations, and others by community hospitals.

There are others to whom I would like to express my appreciation. Among those who helped along the way are Chris Atchison, Mary Weaver, and Janan Wunsch of the Iowa Department of Public Health; students who cared (such as Tina Emerson and Brett Long), and Marge Garlow, who added her significant organizational skills to the project. I am indebted to several deans of The University of Iowa College of Medicine, particularly James Clifton, who encouraged me to pursue research, scholarship, and relevance wherever it might take me. Most important were the good will and support of the community leaders who allowed an academic into their health systems.

James E. Rohrer, PhD
Professor
Graduate Program in Hospital
and Health Administration
College of Medicine
The University of Iowa
Iowa City, Iowa

Table of Contents

Chapter 1

Planning Doctrine

STRATEGIC MANAGEMENT OF COMMUNITY HEALTH, which is usually called community health planning, has never taken root in the United States. Public health professionals advocate and practice community health planning, and examples of successful planning efforts abound. On the other hand, planning projects are difficult to initiate and execute, and they often leave no lasting impression on the health system. In an era of managed care involving profit-seeking competition, the relevance of community-oriented planning may seem to be very much in doubt. However, planning has seldom been more needed or more useful, or so I shall argue in this book.

Explanations for the lack of acceptance of community health planning are close at hand. Because of its association with local and state government, many Americans are automatically suspicious of it. Proponents of coordination fight an uphill battle in a culture that is ideologically predisposed in favor of market competition. Policy makers often demonstrate their own lack of commitment by providing neither resources nor public enthusiasm for local planning projects. And, of course, health professionals (both medical and public health) frequently resist coordinated action because they fear loss of autonomy.

Yet community health planning is needed, and it can be implemented successfully. Public support is difficult to mobilize for reasons related to basic cultural values and assumptions. However, some strongly held values can be supportive of planning initiatives. The challenge is to tap into those values directly. Meeting this challenge may require recrafting doctrine and metaphor as they are employed by planners. I will address these issues by first gleaning relevant insights from the regional planning and community development fields. First, however, it is necessary to clarify the definition of community health planning.

Definitions

Community Health Planning Defined

Community health planning has generally been regarded as a public health function because its goal is community health, it has a population focus, it draws on epidemiology, and, most important, only public health rises above diverse private interests for the common good. I am assuming here that public health means not just government health programs but any activity by any agency that seeks to enhance community health.

Though health planning is a public health activity, not all health planners come from public health backgrounds. In general, planners, managers, and policy analysts differ not in the content of their professional preparation or in their skills but in their personal ideological orientations and where they as individuals want to focus their attention.[1] All three must be able to work with limitations on their authority, building consensus where possible. In their degree programs, all three are exposed to management theory, economics, sociology, statistical methods, and the like. All three fields blend hard and soft data, facts and intuition. But managers identify with other managers, planners with their peers, and policy analysts with theirs.

Correspondingly, planning, managing, and policy analysis involve similar activities. Managing a community health system requires planning, organizing, and evaluating progress. Planners perform the same functions, as do policy analysts. Therefore, the important information contained in the phrase "community health planning" is not in the word "planning," since the process could just as easily be called management of community health or development of community health policy. The important words are "community" and "health." Community health activities relate to keeping community members healthy and preventing disease progression as well as treating the sick. Community health planning also relates to all sectors of the community. Private enterprise, government, interest groups, health professionals, and consumers are all included in the concept of community. Since communities can be the focus of attention in regional and state health planning, community health planning can be said to occur at all levels.

Doctrine and Metaphor

Regional or urban planning is a field with which public health has had little commerce. However, the problems encountered and processes employed in city planning are similar to what happens in community health planning. The insights provided by urban planners have provocative implications for community health planners.

An interesting example is found in Faludi and van der Valk's study of Dutch planning.[2] Given a shortage of dry land, the Dutch have done an impressive job of protecting their environment from urban sprawl. Dutch planners have been aided by the existence of planning doctrine that is held in common, gives coherence to their efforts, and avoids the need to revisit basic issues in every planning situation. Doctrine provides general goals, strategies, and principles, leaving planners free to concentrate on understanding how plans must be tailored to local circumstances.

At times, planning may drift into technocracy, where planners assume they know best what should be done in each community. Technocratic planning can be contrasted with sociocratic planning, which is participative and responsive to coalitions of concerned groups.[2] Contemporary doctrine subscribes to the sociocratic perspective, but this is not a new idea.

Doctrine is a vehicle by which consensus is maintained. Doctrine contains self-evident truths contributing to emotional security, self-confidence, and decentralized management. However, an element of faith supports doctrine; rational arguments are contained in it, but they are supportive rather than essential.

Planning doctrine is defined as interrelated and durable notions about spatial arrangements in an area, development of that area, and the process by which arrangements are made and development is handled. A principle of spatial organization is needed. In Holland, the Green Heart is that principle.[2] The Green Heart is a metropolitan park surrounded by urban development. The Green Heart metaphor evokes pastoral reminiscences and generates emotional support for the operative principle of spatial organization (i.e., central park areas are essential to quality of life and therefore take precedence in urban development plans). Clearly, the planning metaphor can be a powerful vehicle for generating and maintaining consensus.

Styles of Planning and the Possibility of Social Progress

Three models of community health organizing can be identified.[3] The *social planning model* relies on rational management. Steps include fact finding, problem definition, goal setting, implementation, monitoring, feedback, and evaluation. In its pure form, it is highly technocratic. In contrast, the *community development model* is characterized by education for participation and development of local leadership. Consensus development and a participative process are more important than action or results. In the activist model, social action is achieved by mobilizing threatened groups around a particular issue. Conflict is not avoided and may be a goal.

Each of these models has its weaknesses. Indeed, postmodernists are critical of all three.[3] The possibility of expert knowledge is doubtful, activists who are not local are to be suspected, and calls for justice sound rather dogmatic. Some critics question the very possibility of social progress; others specifically see economic development as being socially destructive.[4]

These perspectives may turn apathy into a virtue. However, some positive values remain even among the most nihilistic intellectuals. The concept of community generates fierce support from both left and right and may be the value community health planners can use to mobilize support.

Doctrine and Metaphor in Health Planning

In the foregoing discussion the argument is made that both doctrine and metaphor are necessary for health planning to take root. Health planning has both, but they require examination in order to identify why they do not have the same compelling effect found in the Green Heart. In the next section I will review the standard planning doctrine implicitly employed in the United States. In the following section, I will address the difficult task of developing a metaphor for community health planning.

Special Characteristics of the Health Care Market

The recent development of the health care delivery system can be divided into three eras, each characterized by its own paradigm. In the first era, providers were reimbursed for their services without question. Their individual professionalism was seen as sufficient to guarantee good performance in the aggregate. By the 1980s, the professional dominance era had given way to a competitive era. Payers, both business and government, had concluded that each payer should use market power to arrange the most prudent purchase possible. Competition among purchasers and among providers was expected to generate sufficient incentives to ensure acceptable performance.

The competitive market era is giving way now to an era of managed care. Managed care plans can be classified roughly into two categories: those initiated by insurance companies and those initiated by health care providers. While the term "health maintenance organization" (HMO) has been appropriated by insurance-type plans (in fact, HMOs are regulated under insurance statutes), older plans such as Kaiser Permanente see themselves primarily as health care delivery systems and secondarily as insurance plans. Regardless of where managed care is initiated, however, the goal is to achieve control over health care delivery by integrating it with the financing system and thus putting providers at risk for the financial consequences of patient care decisions. Under these arrangements, enhancement of community health may reduce costs; public health functions can become good business, unless excluding certain social groups offers greater potential for profit. It is also possible, however, for managed care companies to seek short-term profits at the expense of community health. Therefore, public oversight to ensure accountability is necessary. Monitoring health system performance is a public health function in which planners play a central role. Indeed, planning can be defined as managing a market to ensure accountability.

Policies that interfere with the market for personal health services or that permit anticompetitive behavior can be justified on the basis of three premises. First, deficiencies in the market for such services result in suboptimal performance of that market. In other words, affordable and effective health services are not always available when needed. Second, suboptimal performance is less acceptable in health services than it would be in other industries, because the public's health is at stake. Third, these problems are correctable through better system design. The third point will be discussed later in this chapter. The second point is a value statement shared by many but not all Americans; it will be regarded as a valid assumption. Here I will review why the market for health services research has what have been called "special characteristics" that explain why it frequently fails to deliver personal health services at reasonable prices and in desired quantities.[5] The theoretical basis for market failure is found in the nature of both demand and supply factors.

The Demand Side: Consumers

Deficiencies in health care markets fall into two categories: those resulting from a tendency toward monopoly and those resulting from consumer irrationality. Neoclassical microeconomic theory assumes that rational consumers are necessary to make markets work, because suppliers will not provide the services people want unless they are rewarded for doing so. Theoretically, rational consumers can provide that reward by purchasing services from the responsive producer. However, when consumers do not shop intelligently, then producers are not rewarded; if good work does not pay off, they may as well do shoddy work. In short, competition will not result in efficient production of services people want unless consumers make intelligent purchases.

While the amount of intelligent shopping for health services has increased, several barriers to rationality remain. The first relates to lack of information: health services are difficult to shop for because people often do not know what services are most appropriate for their health problems. That is why they go to an agent—the physician—for guidance. Consumers cannot easily shop for physicians on the basis of price and effectiveness, because information about medical effectiveness is difficult to obtain and interpret. Furthermore, decisions about health services are often made under emotional duress, which reduces the client's ability to make rational decisions.

In short, the consumer is dependent on his or her personal physician to offer advice about what services to purchase. This makes the ethics and competence of the physician a consumer concern. In the past, local medical societies were trusted to deal with these matters. Working against them, however, was the way we in the United States have traditionally paid for medical care. Physicians are reimbursed for most services by insurance companies. This used to mean that they got paid more for doing more and that their clients did not have to pay much for the service, although rising consumer copayments in the 1980s changed the latter point. The situation created the opportunity and incentive for doctors to err on the side of overtreatment without hurting clients financially. However, a new era is here now.

The Demand Side: Managed Care

Because overtreatment appears to be very common in the United States, the cost of insurance is high, prompting large employers who purchase group health insurance plans to demand better management of care. While insurance companies try to manage doctors (who are not their employees) or designate parsimonious doctors as "preferred providers," the employers shop for insurance companies that can offer lower rates. The net effect is that the market for health care revolves not around the purchase of medical services by clients but around the purchase of services by insurance companies and the purchase of insurance by employers.

As a result of these changes, the rationality of the consumer is becoming a moot question. What will matter, in regard to making the market work, is whether insurance companies and employee benefit managers can shop intelligently. Since they can employ experts who are not personally involved in the illness, these organizations may become better equipped to make sound decisions than individual consumers have been. However, even the experts have trouble discerning inappropriate treatment. And when preferred providers are selected, motivating the consumer to use them can be difficult. Perhaps most important, a market driven by insurance companies and employers does not meet the needs of the uninsured. This point is the motivating force behind much government health planning activity.

In fact, reimbursement is the key to access for the nonpoor as well. Private and public insurance plans often do not fully cover some potentially valuable services, such as primary care, home care, and preventive care. Managed care companies attempt to control utilization of all services, especially those whose efficacy has been questioned (e.g., mental health and substance abuse treatment and many high-tech interventions). Consumers do not want to pay for such services out of pocket, and, as a result, providers do not produce them. The net effect is a health care system that tends to invest in acute care capacity rather than primary care, preventive services, and behavioral health services.

The Supply Side: Managed Care

The discussion to this point has addressed the demand side of the market for health services, that is, consumer rationality. Also at issue is the supply side. Both rational consumers and responsive providers are needed to make a competitive market work. The likelihood that the system of providers will respond automatically to demands for affordable and effective personal health services available when needed is small, because of the tendency toward monopoly.

Some industries tend to become monopolistic or oligopolistic. This is because significant economies of scale, economies of scope, economies of distribution, management improvements, or transaction cost savings can be achieved by investing in larger production facilities and by vertical integration.[6-11] Smaller firms are forced out of business because their costs are higher, and new entrants to the market are discouraged because a very large initial investment is required.

Managed care is an example of vertical integration. When health care delivery systems offer insurance to enrollees, they put themselves at financial risk for the costs of their decisions. This can be called integration because two functions originally separate (delivery and financing) are now combined in one organization. The consequence of such integration is a powerful incentive to control health care costs. Partial integration in the form of a close relationship with clear contractual expectations is more common. We might expect that coordination costs would be higher and cost control less powerful under insurance-initiated managed care, since it is one step removed from complete integration. However, insufficient research evidence exists to confirm this point.

The Supply Side: Producers

The hospital industry is an industry that tends to have few producers in local markets. Only a few hospitals are needed in each region, since each one requires a large investment in buildings, equipment, and personnel. A single hospital may enjoy a monopoly in a rural area, and only a few hospitals are found in most cities under 500 000 in population. In short, there are demographic limits to the amount of competition that can occur in some areas.[12]

Community hospital care can become concentrated (provided by only a few firms) because production and distribution are cheaper for larger, more diversified firms. Economies of scale are achievable in most types of hospital services. Surgery, for example, is provided in operating rooms (ORs). ORs must be cleaned and resupplied after each procedure and the staff who use them command high salaries. These resources can be more fully utilized if the hospital has several ORs. This permits the OR staff to perform many more procedures each day than they otherwise would be able to do. People who need surgery unexpectedly are more likely to find an OR available. And since only a certain number of surgeries are needed in a given city, only a few OR suites will be required.

Economies of scope also occur in hospitals. When a hospital is equipped to perform appendectomies and cesarean sections, for example, the marginal cost of preparing to do other kinds of surgery is small. When a hospital establishes the capacity for providing nursing care for internal medicine patients, adding a specialty ward is not very difficult compared with starting a hospital from scratch.

Vertical integration promotes transaction costs savings. Some hospitals not equipped to perform certain laboratory functions purchase them from a private laboratory. The hospital may have to pay high prices to the private laboratory or engage in an effort to locate cheaper services. It will, of course, be necessary to monitor the quality of the services purchased as well as the price. These transaction costs may be reduced if the hospital extends the capabilities of its own laboratory.

Vertical integration also reduces distribution costs. Hospitals must market their services, and many are forced to compete for the attention of physicians and potential clients. Advertising costs are incurred, and special benefits may have to be offered to physicians to keep them happy. However, if the hospital can purchase physicians' practices and thus guarantee a stream of admissions, then distribution costs are reduced.

Finally, size permits investment in managerial resources useful for standardization of operations. Performance monitoring systems can reduce inefficiency and improve quality, but they require large investments in software, equipment, and specially trained personnel.

In short, economies in production and distribution accrue to hospitals that grow. There are, of course, limits to how large a hospital can be before it begins to incur diseconomies of scale and scope. Therefore, we are not likely to ever find ourselves facing a hospital industry with only one giant facility in each state.

Another reason the size of hospitals is limited is the local nature of hospital markets. Some people will travel great distances for hospital care. Most will travel for urgently needed care if they must and if they have sufficient time and money to make the trip. However, consumers tend to prefer local hospitals for most services, for convenience and because hospital care may be needed immediately. As a result, community hospitals do not face much competition for basic services from hospitals in other cities unless those sites are nearby. Another result of consumers' preference for local hospitals is that there is no benefit in allowing a single hospital to grow larger than it needs to be to produce the quantity of services demanded in its own region. However, by coalescing into systems single hospitals gain economies such as those arising from improved management.

Physician services may also tend toward monopoly. Only two or three doctors are needed in many communities, and they can gain advantages by forming a partnership. Organized group practices are probably both more efficient and more effective than dispersion of physicians into many solo practices. Peer review becomes possible and thus the quality of care may improve. Organization into systems may also improve the performance of emergency medical care providers and nursing homes. Since most small communities do not need more than one or two organized group practices, monopolistic markets can easily develop.

Industries that tend toward monopoly are characterized by certain pathologies. Since they face little or no competition, they may be free to charge high prices, produce less than consumers want of some services and more than they want of others, and deliver shoddy products. Sole producers of vital services may also gain political power, which they can use to further solidify their market niches.

Despite these advantages, producers in monopolistic industries experience economic difficulties. Railroads, power companies, and hospitals, when unregulated, have all exhibited a tendency to overinvest relative to market demand. Evidence of hospital overinvestment can be found in low hospital occupancy rates. A study of the hospital system in Oregon found 238 unnecessary hospital beds, which could have been closed for a savings of $47.3 million.[13] A similar analysis in Iowa found that 60% of hospital beds were not needed.[14] Overinvestment of this type occurs because each of the small number of competitors is seeking to gain the various economies associated with larger productive capacity. The net result may be inefficiency, as producers struggle to cover high fixed costs with low volumes, or destructive dislocations, which can occur when major producers go bankrupt. The hospitals that go out of business may not be the ones least needed—those serving the poor, minorities, and rural populations may be financially the weakest and thus most vulnerable.

These pathologies are the justification for health planning. Planners seek to compare industry performance with ideal performance and propose corrections where necessary. Because hospital care is the most expensive dimension of the nation's health bill, hospitals have been the focus of attention for many planners. However, other types of health services also require the intervention of planners.

Organizational Design Principles

The purpose of this section is to identify organizational characteristics affecting the performance of local health care delivery systems. In order to do so, it will be necessary to consider hypotheses generated by organizational theorists and the empirical findings of health services researchers. This will lead us to the theory supporting capitated financing of services, delivered by vertically integrated systems that control and coordinate all levels of care (regionalization).

In 1932, a blue-ribbon panel called the Committee on the Costs of Medical Care recommended the organization of local health care delivery into hospital-based group practices, financed by prepayment and controlled by health planning.[15] Those recommendations are consistent with organization theory as applied to health care. Indeed, the work of the Committee has stood the test of time better than almost any other contribution to the health services research literature.

One of the most important characteristics of modern society is that management has been used to improve organizational performance, a phenomenon that has fundamentally changed the structure of modern society. Large corporations have replaced small businesses, governments have assumed responsibilities formerly left to individuals, and individuals contract with attorneys, physicians, accountants, and social workers for the management of their personal affairs.

These changes reflect a widespread belief in the basic principles of classical management. These include the following: (1) specialization increases performance; (2) the activities of specialists must be coordinated if they are to optimize organizational objectives; and (3) effective coordination depends on giving a single manager a general knowledge of how the specialists' work ultimately aids in accomplishing organizational objectives, timely and accurate information about the performance of the various specialists, and the authority to influence the behavior of the specialists. The net result of implementing these principles is the creation of hierarchical organizations in which work is allocated, monitored, and controlled as rationally as possible.

If we assume that management really can improve organizational performance, then organization theorists may conclude that the system of health care delivery should be managed as if it were an organization, especially since it apparently does not function well as a market. Managing a market is called planning. A key question now becomes, For what purpose is a market managed—for profit, growth, or improvements in health?

HMOs as Optimal Design

The principles of management presented above are distilled from classical organization theory. More recent work is somewhat different in flavor, but close examination reveals its origins in classical theory. Freidson's theory on the organization of medical practice is a good example. Freidson assumed that the structure of the work setting influences individual behavior.[16] A physician in solo practice might perform poorly for an indefinite period of time because he or she is not being supervised by anyone else. When a physician enters into a partnership, the chance that errors will be noticed increases. Partners may be interested in monitoring each other's practice when they share financial or legal risk. When a larger group practice forms, the characteristics of a bureaucracy (specialization, coordination and record keeping) will begin to emerge. Peer review, consultation, substitution of physician extenders, and economies of scale can be achieved. When the group practice becomes fully organized, physicians are employees of the organization. Thus the physician-manager has responsibility for the performance of staff physicians and the authority to control it. The organization also has the incentive to control efficiency when the group practice is prepaid, as in an HMO. Therefore, the highest level of structure would be expected in a staff model HMO, and the best performance.

Newer types of managed care organizations may not perform as well as staff or group model HMOs, because they lack the same degree of control over patient care. However, Robert Miller and Harold Luft note the development of "network based" managed care, which will give some non-HMO managed care organizations almost as much economic leverage as HMOs.[11] The principle remains the same: More control is better.

The risk, of course, is that enhanced control will be used to reap short-term profits rather than to enhance community health. Community health could be dramatically damaged if delivery systems are not held accountable for their performance. This can be accomplished, in theory, through public oversight, sound governing bodies, or both.

Physicians, Hospitals, and Vertical Integration

Most community hospitals can be described as quasi firms because, although the medical staff and the hospital have common purposes, they are only loosely coupled.[7] The typical physician is an independent businessperson who agrees to cooperate with a hospital in exchange for access to hospital resources. Managers have some controls over physicians, but not as many as they have over employees. The degree to which hospitals and physicians are formally linked may be the most important variable to considering when classifying hospitals, because such linkages mean that doctors and hospitals can work in a coordinated fashion to maximize system performance. Integrated health systems, common in larger metro areas, have salaried physician employees, and these systems own and operate multiple physician offices.

Also important is the array of services a hospital offers. This is especially relevant when the hospital's performance in meeting community needs is considered, rather than just its internal efficiency and effectiveness. For example, a hospital may have low production costs and high quality. However, if the community needs primary care and the hospital does not offer it, then its effectiveness is necessarily limited. In fact, the hospital may be inappropriately overservicing the community in its major product lines and at the same time inappropriately underservicing the community in primary care.

Ideally, prepaid organized group practices are linked with hospitals offering a basic level of services. These basic primary care hospitals are formally affiliated with secondary facilities offering more specialized services. Finally, a group of secondary care hospitals has formalized referral arrangements with tertiary care hospitals. Both secondary and tertiary care hospitals also provide lower levels of care to local consumers. The entire vertically integrated structure is called a regionalized health care delivery system.

Regionalized systems permit increased coordination among the levels of care. They also achieve economies of scale and reduced transaction costs. By not permitting duplicate investments in competing facilities, regionalized systems reduce overhead costs. Finally, since competition tends to raise costs in health care by increasing the quantity of services delivered, regionalization (which reduces competition) leads to a substantially lower cost of care per capita.

Regionalized health care has been considered ideal since publication of the Dawson Report in 1920. The model still has proponents, as evidenced by the American Hospital Association's advocacy of regional systems in 1992.[17] The Association's concept of "community care networks" specifies the organization of hospitals, physicians, and other providers into capitated, hierarchically ordered networks.

The building blocks of regional systems are their component primary care systems. To be fully effective and efficient, local primary care systems should be organized into community health networks that

- are community based;
- ensure collaborative relationships between local or regional providers;
- provide integration of the full range of services, with an emphasis on early intervention, disease prevention and primary care, to residents of the community served;
- provide health promotion services, including community outreach and incentives for the appropriate utilization of such services targeted to meet special community health needs as identified by regular assessments of community health status;
- demonstrate accountability to the community by, at a minimum, including public health and other community leaders in the governing board and providing regular reports on health outcomes, costs, timeliness of service, and other measures of quality;
- secure geographic accessibility to all individuals residing in the area served, without social, cultural, communication, or other barriers to health care;

- incorporate continuing health education and health professional training with an emphasis on community-based primary and preventive health care; and
- incorporate methods for evaluation of health outcomes addressing identified community health needs.

A Metaphor for Community Health Planning

For many years health planners have been driven by their knowledge of the special characteristics of the health care market and organizational design principles to a vision of regionalized health system organization. A regionalized health system is organized around tertiary care centers. Community hospitals are linked to the tertiary care center for specialized services they cannot deliver safely or effectively. Several primary care centers and long-term care facilities are linked to the community hospitals.

The metaphor of the regionalized system casts the tertiary care center in the central role. It is the hub of a wheel that is surrounded by smaller wheels. The primary care centers are at the periphery. Patients flow to the center for more sophisticated care, then back out to lower levels of care. Resources are concentrated at the hubs because of the capital investment required for tertiary services.

The problem with this metaphor is that it devalues primary care by placing it at the periphery. Yet a community-based health care system is grounded in primary care. Primary care is what most people need most of the time. Sufficient resources must be invested in primary care to ensure adequate care, accurate diagnoses, and appropriate referrals to community hospitals. And the only way to ensure the primacy of primary care is to place the governing authority at the local level (see Figure 1.1). Each primary care system should have its own governing board. The primary care boards could be linked to each other to create a corporate board that, in turn, would treat community hospitals and tertiary care centers as support services, rather than the other way around.

Such a structure is not likely to emerge, at least not in the short run. Nevertheless, it gives rise to a useful metaphor—a flower. The petals (types of primary care and prevention services)

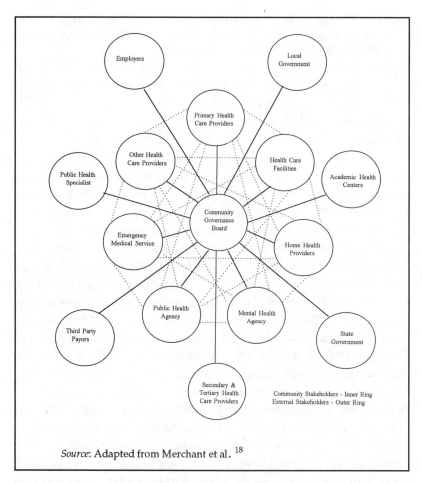

Source: Adapted from Merchant et al. [18]

FIGURE 1.1. The community–based health network.

are coordinated at the local level by the center of the flower. The stalk leads down to secondary and tertiary care levels, which hold up the flower, being clearly subordinate. Perhaps this metaphor will help us keep a perspective consistent with the design and evaluation of community health systems.

Conclusion

Planning doctrine emerges from theory in the form of certain guiding assumptions:

- Health care systems should emphasize primary care and prevention.
- Health care should be organized into regionalized systems.
- Health care systems should be capitated.

Respect for these assumptions should, in theory, lead to better performance on the part of the delivery system. Worse performance would be expected when there is overinvestment in hospital care and competition among care providers. None of these assumptions may prove to be sound in particular situations. Therefore, the planner must continually monitor system performance and be prepared to recommend changes in design.

This perspective is captured in Figure 1.2. Planning doctrine calls for grounding the local health care delivery system in community needs, which requires that needs assessment be the first step in strategic planning (upper left quadrant of figure). The delivery system is organized to meet community needs, drawing from planning doctrine for design principles (upper right quadrant). The performance of providers is addressed on an ongoing basis (lower right quadrant), primarily in terms of appropriateness and quality of the care provided. Overall system performance (lower left quadrant) must be assessed in order to verify that it is meeting community needs; this is how accountability is established. Accountability is so important that it might easily be included in the needs assessment.

Taken in its entirety, Figure 1.2 captures the definition of community-oriented health systems planning. Several types of evaluation are required for planning; it is assumed here that evaluation is part of the planning process. The next several chapters of the book address how the planner might go about conducting the steps indicated in the figure: systems design (chapter 2), needs assessment (chapter 3), system performance assessment (chapter 4), and organizational performance assessment (chapter 5).

REFERENCES

1. Benveniste G. *Mastering the politics of planning*. San Francisco, Calif: Jossey-Bass; 1989.
2. Faludi A, van der Valk A. *Rule and Order: Dutch Planning Doctrine*

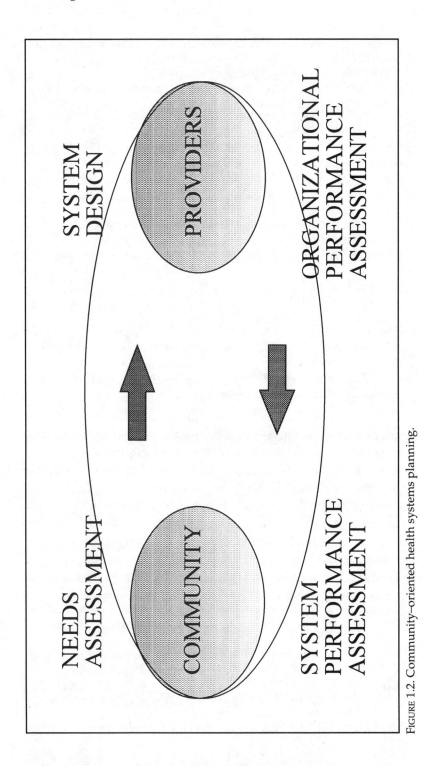

FIGURE 1.2. Community–oriented health systems planning.

   in the Twentieth Century. Dordrecht, The Netherlands: Kluwer
   Academic Publishers; 1994.

3. Rosenau PV. Health politics meets post-modernism: its meaning
   and implications for community health organizing. *J Health Polit
   Policy Law.* 1994;19:303–333.

4. Lasch C. *The Revolt of the Elites and the Betrayal of Democracy.* New
   York, NY: WW Norton & Co Inc; 1995.

5. Donabedian A. *Aspects of Medical Care Administration.* Cambridge,
   Mass: Harvard University Press; 1973.

6. Hurley RE. The purchaser-driven reformation in health care:
   alternative approaches to leveling our cathedrals. *Front Health Serv
   Manage.* 1993;9(4):5–35.

7. Begun JW, Luke RD, Pointer DD. Structure and strategy in hospital-
   physician relationships. In: Mick SS & Associates, eds. *Innovations
   in Health Care Delivery.* San Francisco, Calif: Jossey-Bass; 1990:116–
   143.

8. Conrad DA, Mick SS, Madden CW, Hoare G. Vertical structures
   and control in health care markets: a conceptual framework and
   empirical review. *Med Care Rev.* 1988;45:49–100.

9. Harris C, Hicks LL, Kelly BJ. Physician-hospital networking:
   avoiding a shotgun wedding. *Health Care Manage Rev.* 1992;17(4):17–
   28.

10. Luke RD. Local hospital systems: forerunners of regional systems?
    Front Health Serv Manage. 1992;9(2):3–51.

11. Miller RH, Luft JS. Managed care: past evidence and potential
    trends. *Front Health Serv Manage.* 1993;9(3):3–37.

12. Kronick R, Goodman DC, Wennberg J, Wagner E. The marketplace
    in health care reform. *N Engl J Med.* 1993;28:148–152.

13. Fisher ES, Welch HG, Wennberg JE. Prioritizing Oregon's hospital
    resources. *JAMA.* 1992;267:1925–1931.

14. Hilsenrath P, Chien R, Rohrer JE. Implementing EACHs and PCHs
    on a state-wide basis: a preliminary assessment. *J Rural Health.* 1991;
    7:618–629.

15. Committee on the Costs of Medical Care. *Medical Care for the
    American People.* Chicago, Ill: University of Chicago Press; 1932.

16. Freidson E. Profession of Medicine: A Study of the Sociology of
    Applied Knowledge. New York, NY: Harper & Row, 1970.

17. American Hospital Association. Key concepts underlying AHA's
    national health care reform strategy. Mimeograph. Chicago, Ill;
    1992.

18. Merchant JA, Rohrer JE, Walkner LM, Urdaneta ME. *Provision of
    Comprehensive Health Care to Rural Iowans in the 21st Century.* PEW
    Charitable Trusts and The Robert Wood Johnson Foundation Health
    of the Public Report. Iowa City, Iowa: University of Iowa; 1994.

Chapter 2

Designing Community Health Systems

MARKET CHANGE IN HEALTH CARE DELIVERY is proceeding at a breathtaking pace, which should cause the reader to approach this book with a certain degree of skepticism. Turbulent times are always rife with risk for those who would advise others how to prepare for the future. During the 1980s and 1990s, health care managers have been advised to approach their roles in as businesslike a fashion as possible. Intense competition has been the justification for this advice and possibly, at least partly, a result of it. Regardless of cost and effect, health care delivery has been very competitive and managers have been businesslike.

Properly viewed, this recent period in our history is clearly an aberration. Health care is a local affair, and in most local markets competition, in primary care at least, requires unnecessary duplication of resources. More important, perhaps, competition among local health care providers causes the public to view health care managers with a certain degree of cynicism. After all, if health care providers will aggressively battle each other over revenues, what might they do to the unsuspecting patient if the opportunity for profit presents itself?

Communities would rather trust their health care delivery systems. Often they view them as essential public services, like the school system, fire department, and police protection, even though significant elements are privately owned. This attitude, where found, is a cultural imperative that dictates that a sincere community service mission be adopted by the delivery system. Economic realities in the form of production efficiencies associated with a natural monopoly reinforce this conclusion. This point should be underscored: even profit-oriented health care providers can function in a community-oriented health system, because the local businesses and consumers who purchase services can exchange their patronage for accountability.

21

Grounding the local health care system in community service has important implications. These include the following

- The delivery system should seek to enhance community health.
- The system should be frugal, because communities do not appreciate ostentatiousness or wasted resources in their public services.
- The critical health care delivery organization is not a physical institution such as a hospital, nursing home, or group practice, but a local system of primary care (i.e., a community health network).
- The mission of the local health care system is not a matter of strategic choice. Instead, the mission must be optimization of community health. This requires an emphasis on primary care, health promotion and prevention, and coordination with public health agencies.
- Alternative structures for community-based health systems are more similar than they are different. Key concepts are vertical integration, community-oriented primary care, community governance, population-based planning, and information systems that demonstrate accountability.

The effective health care organization of the future will embrace a mission of community service. Primary care and prevention will be the services around which production processes will be organized. Collaboration among providers will be vital to successful performance. Achieving all this will require substantial change, but there are models to follow. The discussion to follow will provide some ideas on how to proceed.

Mission

The strategic management literature is replete with discussions of strategic behavior. Some organizations are prospectors, frequently searching for new market opportunities. Others are analyzers that stick to their core operations but watch for new opportunities. Defenders rarely innovate and reactors make changes only when forced to do so.[1] This body of literature implies that the leaders of health care organizations are largely free to decide what their organizations will do.

While descriptions of strategic behavior are of academic value, what practicing managers require is a set of prescriptions. Prescriptions are assertions about what to do. Once they are on the table, along with the rationales that support them, managers can accept, modify, or reject them.

In keeping with this perspective, let me observe that the first goal of every health services system is to optimize the health of the population by employing the most advanced knowledge about the causation of disease, illness management, and health maximization.[2] This goal is not a matter of strategic choice. Health care organizations that choose to do otherwise declare themselves peripheral to the health care system and risk losing both legitimacy and community support. That some health care providers have ignored this reality in the pursuit of patients, prestige, or profit is irrelevant. After all, the health care system in our country is widely understood to be dysfunctional. The socially responsible manager will seek to optimize community health. In a properly structured health care organization, this will also constitute good performance to its governing board.

Given that the purpose of the organization is optimization of community health, the mission statement can be expected to emphasize primary care, health promotion, and disease prevention. Specialty care is essential, but it cannot optimize health because preventing illness and promoting optimal functioning requires a broader perspective than can be achieved by the disease specialist.[2] Effective medical care must take into account the contexts in which the patient lives and works and the full spectrum of health problems he or she has. A generalist, rather than a specialist, is required to integrate specialty services, understand what services the patient requires, and plan prevention strategies.

Primary care includes appropriate treatment of common diseases and injuries, provision of essential drugs, and coordination of specialty care. It also includes maternal and child health programs; prevention of disease; and promotion of sound nutrition, health education, and environmental sanitation. This mix of services will achieve the maximum impact on community health per dollar invested. Thus it is clearly consistent with the goal of the health system and should feature prominently in the mission statement.

Types of Local Primary Care Systems

Local primary care systems can be confused with some other types of health care organizations. The term "primary care network" is often used to mean a horizontally integrated collection of primary care physician practices. Primary care networks may spread over regions comprising several communities. A physician-hospital organization is a partnership between a hospital and its medical staff. The physician-hospital organization is community-specific but may not have a mission oriented toward community health. Since physician-hospital organizations and primary care networks are often formed so that their members can compete for managed care contracts, it is likely that both will eventually organize and deliver services under capitation financing. Capitation payment, from a theoretical perspective, contains incentives that encourage providers to minimize inappropriate care and emphasize prevention programs. However, until providers explicitly adopt optimization of community health as their primary mission, physician-hospital organizations and horizontal primary care networks will not evolve into local primary care systems.

In the 1980s, four basic types of organizational design could be identified for primary care organizations, based on whether they were sponsored by a community board, the public sector, physicians, or a hospital.[3] A community-sponsored organization might be a free clinic, a hospice, or an AIDS program. Typically, such organizations are established because of a perceived failure on the part of health care providers to meet an important need for services. These organizations tend to be small and informal.

A public-sector primary care program typically has what is known as a machine structure. Clear job descriptions exist for personnel and organizational units. For example, the primary care physician does not do community health nursing, and the nurse does not worry about environmental sanitation. This division of labor reduces flexibility but can increase effectiveness in specialized areas. Attention must be directed toward coordinating the separate units. This, of course, is the role of the professional administrator (if the organization can afford one), who reports to a governing board such as the board of health.

In a typical physician-sponsored primary care program, the administrator (often an office manager) reports to the medical staff. Support staff, such as registered nurses, nurse practitioners, physician's assistants, laboratory technicians, and clerical personnel, are accountable to the medical staff either directly or through the administrator. In its most traditional guise, this structure maximizes clinical oversight but does not achieve the benefits possible with a team of health professionals.

Finally, a hospital-sponsored primary care program may simply consist of an outpatient department in which specialty visits are scheduled; an emergency department, which handles patients who do not have a personal physician; or a branch clinic established to generate inpatient referrals. Naturally, these programs will not begin to achieve the performance of a proactive organization that is truly committed to optimizing the health of the community.

The four types of primary care organizations described above still predominate in most local health care systems. Many communities have all four types, sometimes several of each. Smaller communities may have less than the full set. The limitations of each type do not offset each other with any degree of reliability, resulting in local health systems that are uncoordinated, inefficient, and ineffective.

Another perspective on types of primary care organizations was developed by investigators from the Health Services Research Center at the University of North Carolina.[4] These researchers focused on subsidized rural programs, but their ideas are relevant to the general questions of how to organize primary care. They asserted that three relatively stable program characteristics are most important: (1) sponsorship or governance, (2) size and mix of staff, and (3) number of sites. Five forms emerged for them: (1) *traditional solo or other forms of practice*; (2) *satellite practices* (called extension practices by the investigators) controlled by a larger institution such as a health department, private medical practice, hospital, or medical school; (3) *primary care centers* that are independent of larger institutions and are supported by community groups; (4) *organized group practices* having at least two full-time physicians and not providing any outreach services; and (5) *comprehensive health centers* that have a community governing board and at least three full-time primary care providers and that provide outreach services.

As communities struggle to develop coordinated primary care systems, they will be faced with decisions regarding affiliation with vertically integrated networks, which can be defined as self-governing organizations composed of participants that are themselves autonomous organizations or individuals.[5] Complete vertical integration includes secondary and tertiary care and encompasses large geographic areas. Relationships between primary care systems and regional networks will be discussed later in this chapter. The relevance of vertically integrated networks to this discussion lies in the typology of organizational structures used to classify them, since similar dimensions may be relevant to primary care systems.

Moscovice et al. used three dimensions to categorize vertically integrated networks: level of integration, complexity, and assumption of risk.[5] Level of integration is the degree to which the component members function as a single unit. Opposite extremes of this dimension would be represented by an informal network lacking any basis for action other than mutual interest and a single corporation in which all members are subsumed.

Complexity relates to the scope of services offered and the number of partners whose efforts must be coordinated. The simplest primary care system might be a country doctor working alone to deliver all of the primary care needed in a community. At the opposite extreme would be an inner-city community served by a hospital; physicians of several specialties; public health professionals, including community health nurses; a variety of nontraditional health care providers (such as acupuncturists, massage therapists, and chiropractors); and private providers of publicly funded services for vulnerable populations (such as substance abuse treatment programs, community mental health centers, and community health centers). The complexity of the second type of primary care system, which is illustrated in Figure 1.1, is much greater.

Networks also vary in the degree to which they share financial risk. In an informal network the losses of one partner are not shared by the others. Greater risk sharing occurs when the partners agree that losses and profits will be distributed according to some pre-determined formula. Each is motivated to cooperate so as to avoid large losses. The maximum in shared risk is achieved when the partners agree to share the net profit or loss from serving an enrolled population. Providers will each be motivated to achieve a balance of services that avoids use of costly services. Each will seek to maintain patient care volume and control production costs.

Physical integration is another dimension of importance in primary care systems. When partners are housed separately, overhead costs are substantially higher. Furthermore, the ability of each partner to support skilled administrators is more limited than when resources are pooled. Maximum physical integration is achieved when all partners colocate, perhaps on the premises of the local hospital.

Thus, dimensions that describe how primary care systems are organized include sponsorship, organizational integration, complexity, risk-sharing, and physical integration (see Table 2.1). Most communities have not moved very far along any dimension to achieve a higher level of organization.

Fortunately, a few examples can be found of communities where primary care networks have been established that integrated the various components of the local health system. The basic structure of the integrated system is consistent with the theory of community-oriented primary care, described below.

Community-Oriented Primary Care

Community-oriented primary care (COPC) defines and characterizes the community so that the mix of services offered reflects both the common health problems found in the community and social circumstances that influence health. These assessments of community needs are used to modify the primary care program. Program effectiveness is measured not just in terms of impact on patients but also in terms of impact on community health.

To achieve the goal of a health system that is responsive to community needs, the following are required: epidemiological analysis, community governance, and coordination of medical care and other health services with public health programs. Health professionals prefer to be both autonomous and independent, but some degree of cooperation is necessary to optimize community health. Furthermore, health providers

Table 2.1—Typology of Primary Care Systems

Ownership/Sponsorship
       Hospital
       Physician
       Government
       Community
Organizational integration
       Informal
       Formalized
       Single corporation
Complexity
       One type of provider and/or service
       Several types
       All types
Assumption of risk
       None
       Shared profit and loss
       Capitation
Physical integration
       Each partner remains on own premises
       Several partners colocate
       Partners physically work as a team

need community support, and one way to achieve that is with a governing board composed of community leaders including members of the local business community. The business community has a vested interest in cost-effective care, which will help it to control the cost of health benefits for employees. Local government officials also wish to control the cost of health care, since taxes are never popular. Consumers want to be healthy. If providers can satisfy all of these partners, then community support is assured. Since COPC will lead to cost-effective health care, it is in everyone's best interest.

There is no guarantee that COPC will be adopted in many communities, however. As physicians' offices and hospitals become part of regional systems, many of which are owned by profit-seeking investors, insisting on accountability to local needs and concerns may become impossible. The best defense is in close attention to the governance function, discussed later in this chapter. For now, suffice it to say that COPC is an achievable ideal that can lead to rational and cost-effective care, but establishment of such a system may require some David-and-Goliath–type successes.

The degree to which COPC has been achieved in a local system is reflected in four functions: (1) definition and description of the community; (2) identification of community health problems; (3) modification of the health care program; and (4) measurement of program effectiveness.[2] Staging criteria have been developed for each function. A community that fully performs the community definition function has a database enumerating all residents, including address, telephone number, and demographic and socioeconomic data for each individual. Identification of health problems has been fully achieved when priority problems are identified by a community group, the causes of those problems are investigated, and current treatment patterns relating to those problems are documented. Program modification is not being fully performed unless community and public health services, as well as medical care, are appropriately changed. Outreach and targeting of high-risk or priority groups within the community are necessary. Finally, effectiveness monitoring should be determined in light of program objectives, be risk-adjusted, and reveal weaknesses as well as strengths of the program.

The COPC functions described above will remind managers of a generic model of strategic planning: goals and objectives are set on the basis of data and values of the governing body, programs are redirected, and outcomes are judged against predetermined objectives. In order for strategic planning for a primary care network to succeed, no single partner can dominate the process. A common problem is for hospital-based planners to seek to control board membership and priority setting so that the hospital remains important in the local health care system. Even worse, hospital planners may initiate community health planning efforts in an attempt to shore up the role of the hospital in acute inpatient care at the expense of primary care and prevention. The consequence of such an effort is likely to be loss of legitimacy for the network and absence of community support for network initiatives. Hospital planners will have to set aside their natural tendency to want to control events and support acute care in favor of a form of leadership that supports shared goals and promotes primary care.

The fact remains, however, that in many communities the greatest reservoir of managerial experience lies in the local hospital. Leadership from this source may well make the difference in whether the network is successful.

Other sources of leadership can also be found. Both public health departments and community health centers are candidates.[6] Health departments have long been entrusted with assessing health needs and health system performance and developing health-promoting policies.[7] Indeed, public health professionals are likely to be more cognizant of population-based approaches to enhancing community health than are hospital managers. Furthermore, health departments are experienced in working with groups of both public and private providers, and public health centers have provided primary care and prevention services for many years.

Community health centers are also natural leaders in developing a COPC-oriented health system.[6] The 600-plus community health centers, migrant health centers, and homeless health centers in the United States have frequently been identified with COPC. These centers have focused on primary care, been guided by community input, and relied on the full range of health professionals. All three concepts are central to the COPC approach.

Another source of leadership is the academic health center. Public health and medical professionals who practice in academic health centers have great expertise. Furthermore, these centers have money, clinical staff, and education programs that can be brought to bear on local problems. Reform commissions such as that funded by the Pew Foundation have urged academic health centers to shift toward an emphasis on primary care, prevention, population-based medicine, and team practice. The Pew and Robert Wood Johnson foundations funded Health of the Public projects in academic health centers to encourage outreach. The centers are starting to respond. The danger to the local community, of course, is the same as when working with any powerful externally based organization—

ensuring local control. After all, part of what academic health centers do involves marketing specialty services. Business-oriented managers have come to the forefront of academic health center leadership as revenues from specialty care plummet. Academic health centers can and should seek to empower community leaders, but it is always best to clarify local priorities and insist on accountability.

Performance of Primary Care Organizations

During the period 1979 through 1982, subsidized rural primary care clinics were buffeted by a severe recession, high inflation, and significant budget cuts. Despite these difficulties, only 9 out of 193 programs studied actually closed.[8] Programs exhibited adaptiveness and strength in a hostile environment. Interestingly, such programs benefited from being affiliated with hospitals. Both clinic costs and revenue were reduced when clinic providers used the local hospital as a free second office; however, since costs were reduced more than revenues, the financial self-sufficiency of the clinic was enhanced by the relationship.[9]

Clearly, primary care organizations can be durable, especially when they are affiliated with a hospital and receiving some public money. Looking specifically at hospital-sponsored primary care organizations, additional characteristics are also important.[10] A hospital's strong initial commitment to primary care and involving the medical director of the primary care organization in hospital decision-making were important predictors of continued existence. Use of a professional rather than a bureaucratic structure, more visits per full-time equivalent physician, use of residents, and a rural or suburban site were associated with improvements in accessibility of services. Bigger clinics with low physician turnover and rural or suburban sites were more likely to contribute financially to the hospital. The financial performance of the clinic was enhanced by having more commercially insured patients, charging higher prices, having more visits per full-time equivalent physician, offering multiple specialties, using nurse practitioners and/or physician's assistants, and using an incentive compensation plan.

A separate study of a subset of the same sample of community hospital-sponsored group practices provides another perspective on their performance. Community surveys revealed that the hospital-sponsored practices attracted people who had not previously had a regular source of care. Access and satisfaction were good. Use of inpatient services, emergency rooms, and hospital outpatient departments was not increased by the primary care programs. In short, access to primary care was improved without raising costs in other ways. The authors recommended hospital-sponsored primary care programs for underserved areas.

Community Governance

Primary care systems can become more organized as a result of initiatives taken by any of the participants in the system, but the local hospital may be best equipped with managerial expertise (see Example 1). However, since hospital administrators are often oriented toward controlling events, they may find it difficult to play a cooperative role in the development of systems that empower the community even when changing the mission of the hospital is required (see Example 2). Hospital administrators are more likely to approach community governance sincerely when the survival of their institutions is problematic and cooperation is one of the last remaining strategies for salvaging the situation. Representatives of the for-profit health sector will likely be skeptical of such alliances and determine their benefit in terms of

---

EXAMPLE 1—Providing Community Leadership

Ocean County, New Jersey, has a population of 400 000 residing on the shore. Many citizens are seniors, which adds a special dimension to the needs profile of the community.

Mark Pella, president and CEO of Community Medical Center in Toms River, brought together more than 80 community leaders to work on improving the quality of life in Ocean County. An external consultant was hired to facilitate the process. After an initial conference involving all participants, seven work groups were established to study transportation, teen and family issues, domestic violence, and a countywide electronic infrastructure.[11]

bottom-line enhancement or mere marketing and public relations.

Other participants may also want to move cautiously, and for the same reasons (see Example 3). As a result, one is forced to the conclusion that an informal, loosely coupled structure for the system may be the most feasible in many situations. Certainly, examples can be found of local planning boards that work to coordinate their primary care systems even without legal incorporation. In theory, these "value added partnerships" involving local business, public health programs, privately owned entities such as community health centers, and private providers such as physician practices and the hospital can be stable as long as they continue to function in the best interests of their members.[12]

If the local hospital is evolving into the center of a primary care system, then the hospital's board of trustees may be able to grow into a new role as community-oriented system managers. However, the ability of many hospital boards to be progressive has been questioned.[13,14] The creation of a new body called a steering committee, community health planning task force, citizens' committee, or health commission may be necessary.

Community governance begins with a development process. A temporary planning body, composed of represen-

---

EXAMPLE 2—Retaining Control

Smithville is a small town within the service area of Jonesville Medical Center. Jonesville Medical Center has been subsidizing the small hospital in Smithville for several years. Seeing the potential of using community health planning to redirect the Smithville hospital away from acute inpatient care, medical center administrators carefully selected a steering committee in Smithville composed of likely hospital supporters and a few consumers. Only three people attended the first meeting. When asked for an explanation for the low turnout, the attendees observed that the hospital had strategic planning processes, so another one seemed redundant. Furthermore, the planning effort appeared to be a transparent attempt to manipulate the community in a way that would solve the problems facing the hospital, rather than letting the community determine its priorities. Feeling powerless and tricked, most people did not bother to participate.

tatives of all the stakeholders (see Figure 1.1), is established in the hope that it will be sufficiently successful to continue indefinitely. The board should be constituted in a way that will establish its legitimacy in the eyes of the larger community. After all, changes in the health care delivery system are likely to be proposed, which could lead to public outcry. Forcing changes on the community will just lead to consumers' leaving the community for the services they need.

Legitimacy is a delicate issue, and one that requires an insider's knowledge of local politics. Nevertheless, some guidelines can be suggested. First, be sure all of the health providers are represented. Second, do not cast any health provider in a visible leadership role if cynics are likely to interpret the board as a self-serving sham. A local business leader would be an ideal chairperson, provided that the individual has a record of civic leadership. Third, be sure that local government is offered an opportunity to participate. Fourth, involve consumers.

EXAMPLE 3— Letting the Community Set the Pace

A steering committee was established in Monroe County, Iowa, to discuss formation of a local primary care network that could meet the onrushing wave of managed care with clear goals. The committee was composed of representatives from local government, local physicians, the hospital board, hospital administration, the local nursing home, the business community, a major employer, and public health agencies.

At the onset, the group was not willing to commit itself to developing plans relating to managed care. The topic was both emotionally disturbing and technically overwhelming. The committee chose to look at planning data to gain an understanding of health problems in Monroe County. After reviewing a variety of secondary data sources, the steering committee decided that three topics required further investigation: access to primary care for children living in poverty, wellness, and managed care mental health. A community survey was planned to determine consumer perceptions of problems and service needs in these areas. Coordinated implementation of some new initiatives seemed likely. The steering group was evolving into a governing board for a local primary care system.

This last is a difficult issue, since, on the one hand, everyone is a consumer, and on the other hand, people who are consumers without any other connection to the health system are difficult to find. Fifth, keep the local press and state government apprised of planning activities. And finally, use an objective outsider to serve as facilitator and consultant in the development process.

The first task of the newly constituted board will be to set priorities for the local health system. Several methodologies are available to lead the board to a position where it can engage in priority setting. One example is the Assessment Protocol for Excellence in Public Health (APEX-PH), which was developed by the public health community. Any methodology might be appropriate if the board leadership understands that it is engaged in a strategic planning process that will examine data about the health system and interpret the data in light of community values in order to set priorities for the system. (Assembling the data for population-based strategic planning is usually called community assessment. The kinds of information required are discussed in chapter 3.)

Once the board has been educated about the health problems facing the community, it can set priorities for the local health system. These priorities typically emphasize primary care, prevention programs, and emergency services. Task forces can be established to develop programs for addressing priority problems. Performance indicators are also needed so that the degree to which programs are successful can be measured.

The Institute of Medicine has recommended the use of 15 indicators to measure the accessibility of services. These indicators have the force of expert opinion behind them. Also supporting their use is the value of some of them as measures of efficiency and quality as well as access. For example, high hospitalization rates for ambulatory care–sensitive conditions may indicate inefficient use of resources and, possibly, suboptimal care in addition to poor access to primary care. These indicators are discussed in chapters 3 and 4.

Principles for Successful System Development

Developing a primary care system out of the fragmented components present in most communities is a difficult task. Those who have done it successfully suggest that following certain principles will increase the chances for success:

1.   State at the outset that the purpose of planning is to create a shared vision of how the local system can function.[15]

2.   Expand participation beyond health care providers to include the larger community. All relevant constituencies should be represented so that the planning group will be perceived as having legitimacy. An effective chairperson is needed who is neutral and respected and possesses group process skills.[16] Without local leadership, community system development efforts cannot succeed.

3.   Take advantage of internal problems and external threats in a constructive way. For example, financial insolvency of the local hospital or encroachments on the local market from external provider groups can motivate communities to take planning more seriously.[17]

4.   Use a road map for the process. Participants will be reassured and more productive when they understand the sequence of activities.[18] However, the group may not be prepared to think about major system changes when it begins planning under these circumstances. It may be better just to focus on needs assessment and developing a shared vision. The group must be ready for more advanced topics before they are raised, since it can easily balk or even disband.

5.   Rethink the appropriate scope of local health services. The planning group may assume that the historical service mix is reasonable for the future unless challenged to reconsider.[18]

6.   Analyze the health system. All major strengths and weaknesses should be identified to the extent possible. These may include quality of care, local service needs, leadership, financial performance, teamwork, consumer satisfaction, and utilization patterns. Amundson recommends that an outside consultant be used, particularly for the needs assessment.[18]

7.   Provide briefings to the steering committee on key topics.

8.   Use effective group process methods. Experience in conducting meetings, communication, team building, and conflict management can all be helpful.[18]

9.   Commit resources. Communities that are unwilling to invest in a planning process are unlikely to change. Amundson recommends that some local organization be required to put up cash.[18] However, if start- up funds are available from elsewhere, investment of time and energy may be a sufficient commitment from board members.

10.   Continue the planning process. Evaluation of the impact of

implemented plans is necessary; the planning group will need to make changes each year.

11. Take advantage of assistance from larger provider organizations. Sometimes a large hospital system will see primary care system development as being to its advantage. Empowering a community group to serve as a governing board may lead to constructive changes that could never have been forced on the community. For example, when a regional hospital has a management contract with a small hospital that is failing, it may seek to disengage to avoid losses while fearing a backlash from the local physicians, on whom it depends for referrals. Consequently, the regional hospital may choose to subsidize a planning effort without controlling the outcome, in the belief that the result will be goodwill and, possibly, rational restructuring to emphasize primary care.

Integration with Regional Systems

The community health system cannot exist independently of the larger health care system in which it is embedded. Local systems need big partners from whom they can acquire technical expertise and other resources and with whom they can share financial risk.

In 1920, Lord Dawson of Penn presented a white paper on the organization of health services in Great Britain. The report called for three levels of health services: primary health centers, secondary health centers, and teaching hospitals. Formal linkages were needed among these levels of care. This theoretical arrangement has been the basis for regionalized health systems in many countries.[2]

A more recent formulation also proposes three levels of care for regional systems.[19] In the first level, community clinics, each serving about 5000 people and spaced 15 minutes apart, would provide office visits, health education, and pharmacy, laboratory, and x-ray services. Level 2 regional primary care centers, serving about 25 000 people, would add emergency care, mental health services, ambulance service, public health services, periodic specialty clinics, and limited inpatient care.

Another model calls for office care, health promotion, public health, home health, pharmacy, laboratory, specialty clinic, nursing home, and dental services to be coordinated with a primary care hospital providing a few beds for observation and convalescence and serving a population of about 12 000.[20] Regardless of which model of regionalization is employed, it is clear that local primary care practices are the basic building blocks of the regional system. Referral hospitals have no reason to exist beyond supporting the primary care systems in their regions. This should be kept in mind, in light of the natural tendency of referral hospitals to regard themselves as the "hubs" or centers of the system, ultimately dominating regional systems and distorting investments so that referral services are overemphasized. Another danger is that investor-owned systems will dominate to the detriment of local community health.

The key to preventing dominance by the referral hospital, if there is one, is to design the system so that the governing boards of the primary care systems are linked into a regional system board that is distinct from the board of the referral center. One possible way to accomplish this is for the board of the regional system to be primarily composed of representatives of the primary care systems that make up the regional system. The immediate benefit of this design comes into play when revenue declines owing to cuts in government health insurance programs or conversion to closed budgets, as has happened in many communities when aggressive managed care has taken over the market. In the absence of board representation on the part of local systems, managed care could damage local primary care systems by diverting patients out of the community to referral centers for services that could be provided locally.

Therefore, representatives of local systems may be well advised to negotiate for the ability to do some or all of the following as they develop their affiliations with regional systems, whether those systems are controlled by referral hospitals or managed care companies:

1. Maximize use of local primary care providers.
2. Include the services of essential providers such as community mental health centers and substance abuse treatment agencies in the local budget.
3. Offer an insurance product to residents that is "community-rated" (all enrollees pay the same premium, regardless of age or preexisting conditions).

4. Allow open enrollment to the insurance plan, so that those who are ill or have low incomes can benefit from the community rating scheme.

5. Include case management in the budget of the primary care system, so that a case worker can work proactively with high-risk families.

6. Provide assistance to ensure availability of primary care providers. Assistance could be in the form of recruitment, income supports, and relief workers.

7. Arrange for specialty clinics to be provided locally.

8. Offer annual community health outreach programs targeted at priority problems, such as cardiovascular health, prevention of sexually transmitted disease, or drug abuse.

9. Pay malpractice insurance for health care professionals practicing locally.

REFERENCES

1. Shortell SM, Morrison EM, Friedman B. *Strategic Choices for America's Hospitals: Managing Change in Turbulent Times.* San Francisco, Calif: Jossey-Bass; 1990.

2. Starfield B. *Primary care: concept, evaluation, and policy.* New York, NY: Oxford University Press; 1992.

3. Kaluzny AD, Konrad TR. Organizational design and the management of primary care services. In: Bisee GE Jr, ed. *Management of Rural Primary Care: Concepts and Cases.* Chicago, Ill: The Hospital Research and Educational Trust; 1982:31–67.

4. Sheps CG, Wagner EH, Schonfeld WH, et al. An evaluation of subsidized rural primary care programs, I: a typology of practice organizations. *Am J Public Health.* 1983;73:38–49.

5. Moscovice I, Christianson JB, Wellever A. Measuring and evaluating the performance of vertically integrated rural health networks. *J Rural Health.* Winter 1995:9–21.

6. Marcyznski-Music KK. Health care solutions: designing community-based systems that work. San Francisco, Calif: Jossey-Bass; 1994.

7. Institute of Medicine, Committee for the Study of the Future of Public Health. *The Future of Public Health.* Washington, DC: National Academy Press; 1988.

8. Ricketts TC, Guild PA, Sheps CG, Wagner EH. An evaluation of subsidized rural primary care programs, III: stress and survival, 1981–82. *Am J Public Health.* 1984;74:816–819.

9. McLaughlin CP, Ricketts TC, Freund DA, Sheps CG. An evaluation of subsidized rural primary care programs, IV: impact of the rural hospital on clinic self-sufficiency. *Am J Public Health.* 1985;75:749–753.

10. Shortell SM, Wickizer TM, Wheeler JRC. Hospital-sponsored

primary care, I: organizational and financial effects. *Am J Public Health*. 1984;74:784–798.

11. Mycek S. Following the leaders: helping communities take ownership of their health. *Trustee*. 1995;48(3):6–9.

12. Foreman SE, Roberts RD. The power of health care value-adding partnerships: meeting competition through cooperation. In: Levey S, ed. *Hospital Leadership and Accountability*. Ann Arbor, Mich: Health Administration Press; 1992:73–88.

13. Griffith JR. Principles of the well-managed community hospital. In: Levey S, ed. *Hospital Leadership and Accountability*. Ann Arbor, Mich: Health Administration Press; 1992:91–104.

14. Umbdenstock RJ, Hageman WM, Amundson B. The five critical areas for effective governance of not-for-profit hospitals. In: Levey S, ed. *Hospital Leadership and Accountability*. Ann Arbor, Mich: Health Administration Press; 1992:47–58.

15. Van Hook RT, Rosenberg S. Independent networks: future directions. National Rural Health Association. Monograph Series Vol. 6: Alternative models for organizing and delivering health care services in rural areas. Undated.

16. Amundson B, Hagopian A, Robertson DG. Implementing a community-based approach to strengthening rural health services: the community health services development model. WAMI Rural Health Research Center Working Paper Series 11. Seattle, Wash: February 1991.

17. Coddington DC, Moore KD, Fischer EA. *Integrated Health Care: Reorganizing the Physician, Hospital and Health Plan Relationship*. Englewood, Colo: Center for Research in Ambulatory Health Care Administration; 1994.

18. Amundson B. Myth and reality in the rural health service crisis: facing up to community responsibilities. *J Rural Health*. 1993;9(3):176–187.

19. Beaulieu JE, Berry DE, eds. *Rural Health Services: A Management Perspective*. Ann Arbor, Mich: Health Administration Press; 1994.

20. Merchant JA, Rohrer JE, Walkner LM, Urdaneta ME. *Provision of Comprehensive Health Care to Rural Iowans in the 21st Century*. PEW Charitable Trusts and The Robert Wood Johnson Foundation Health of the Public Report. Iowa City, Iowa: University of Iowa; 1994.

Chapter 3

Assessment of Community Needs

▓▓▓▓▓▓ HIS CHAPTER PRESENTS A DETAILED DISCUSSION of how to
▓▓▓ ▓▓▓ estimate resource requirements for hospital services. I
▓▓▓ ▓▓▓ begin with hospitals, not because they are the most
important element in the health system, but because planning
methods are most well developed in regard to hospitals. I will
move on to planning for other types of services after developing
the basic methodology using hospital examples, assuming always
that the managed care era seriously constrains the level of
resources that may be invested in health services. First, however,
the types of needs assessment data will be briefly reviewed.

In accordance with the community-oriented primary
care concept discussed in chapter 2, the primary care network
will base its service mix on community needs. The data required
will revolve around morbidity patterns: From what illnesses do
people suffer? Once morbidity patterns are known, services can
be directed at treating the sick and preventing disease among
those at risk. The planner must always exercise caution, however.
More data are available than can be addressed, leaving open the
possibility that important health problems may be overlooked.
Also, focusing on morbidity could lead planners to emphasize
treatment at the expense of prevention. Nevertheless, the
approach is sound if used carefully.

Unfortunately, morbidity is difficult to measure. The
menu of approaches is as follows:

1. *Demographic and socioeconomic characteristics.* Age, sex, and
race are associated with morbidity rates, so collection of demographic
data about the community can provide insight into service requirements.
Poverty and occupational mix are also useful. Demographic and
socioeconomic data are available from secondary sources, including

Table 3.1—Monroe County Profile: Most Common Causes of Mortality, 1991

	No. of Cases in County
Major cardiovascular disease	58
Heart disease	48
Ischemic heart disease	41
Malignant neoplasms	33
Cerebrovascular disease	8
Pneumonia and influenza	6

Source: National Center for Health Statistics.[1]

the US Census. Unfortunately, complete current information is difficult to assemble for small geographic areas.

2. *Vital statistics.* Population size, birth rates, and death rates by cause (see Table 3.1 for example) are important for obvious reasons: numbers of deaths by cause indicate which illnesses people have.[1] However, many people suffer from acute and chronic diseases that are never listed as causes of death.

3. *Reportable diseases*: Sexually transmitted diseases and infectious childhood diseases are examples of diseases reported by physicians to the health department. Most diseases, however, are not reportable. Some states also have registries of important diseases such as cancer, birth defects, Alzheimer's disease, and trauma. Registries are valuable sources of information about disease prevalence, but their availability and completeness varies by state.

4. *Hospital discharges.* Morbidity patterns can be inferred from the discharge diagnoses of local residents. The most common diagnoses tend to mirror the most common causes of death and may reflect the most common illnesses. In addition, some conditions have been identified as ambulatory care–sensitive, meaning that access to good primary care should keep hospital admissions for these conditions to a minimum. Pediatric asthma is an example of an ambulatory care–sensitive condition. High discharge rates for these conditions imply that attention needs to be directed at the primary care system.Rates of common surgical procedures are also valuable, since higher than expected rates for procedures such as hysterectomy and mastectomy may reflect a weakness in the diagnostic process in the primary care system, a tendency to refer too readily to specialists, or a failure to detect problems early. However, only the most serious cases are hospitalized, so most illnesses are not captured by this data set. Tables 3.2 and 3.3 are

Table 3.2—Monroe County Profile: Most Common Case Types, All Ages, 1992.

Case Type	No. of Admissions
Ambulatory care–sensitive, total	236
Chronic	132
Rapid onset	102
MDC 5—Circulatory systems	242
MDC 14—Pregnancy	157
MDC 15–Newborn/neonate	130
MDC 6—Digestive system	153
MDC 4—Respiratory system	157
MDC 8—Musculoskeletal	137
MDC 1—Nervous system	85
MDC 19—Mental	54

Source: Codman Research Group.[2]

examples of how hospital discharges may be examined.[2] Table 3.2 focuses on which case types are most common in the community, since services must be directed at common problems. Table 3.3 directs attention at how the community compares with state averages, which may serve as benchmarks.

5. *Community perceptions.* Surveys of consumer perceptions about health status; healthy behavior; accessibility, efficiency, and quality of health services; and priorities for the local health system can be conducted. Self-reported morbidity may not be completely accurate, but since perceptions drive behavior, an argument can be made for gathering this information. Unfortunately, no standard community survey form exists, though a useful one is included as an appendix to this volume. Many attempts have been made to gather relevant information without making the form excessively burdensome to complete. The best approach, if a survey is to be conducted, may be to seek guidance from the governing board and community focus group about what kinds of information to collect. For the purposes of the initial community assessment, the board needs to learn about consumer satisfaction with the accessibility of health care services. The board may also want to know where people are going for care and, if they are leaving the local market, why. Health status information may also be collected. However, this information should be obtained from other sources, if possible. The board may also want to learn about the health behaviors of residents. For example, if dietary habits are poor, perhaps

Table 3.3—Monroe County Profile: Selected Case Types Significantly Different from State Averages.

Case Type	Significance Level	No. of Admissions
Total admissions	<.001[a]	1489
Total medical and surgical	<.001[a]	1113
Total medical admissions	<.001[a]	792
Ambulatory Care–Sensitive, total	<.05[a]	236
MDC 14—Pregnancy	<.001[a]	157
MDC 4—Respiratory system	<.05[a]	157
MDC 6—Digestive system	<.05[a]	153
MDC 8—Musculoskeletal	<.05[a]	137
Ambulatory care–sensitive, chronic	<.05[a]	132
MDC 15—Newborn/neonate	<.001[a]	130
MDC 1—Nervous system	<.05[a]	85
Adult Gastroentoritis	<.001[a]	60
MDC 3—Ear, nose, and throat	<.001[a]	48
MDC 9—Skin, breast	<.01[a]	45
Acute myocardial infarction	<.01[a]	40
Adult bronchitis/asthma	<.001[a]	37
Ambulatory care–sensitive, chronic obstructive	<.01[a]	37
Medical back problems	<.001[a]	29
Nutritional and miscellaneous metabolic diseases	<.05[a]	27
Nervous system diseases	<.001[a]	26
Cardiothoracic procedures	<.05[a]	26
Ambulatory care–sensitive, asthma	<.001[a]	25
Adult Pneumonias	<.05[b]	23
Urinary tract stones	<.001[a]	21
Referral–sensitive hip/joint replacement	<.05[b]	20
Psychoses	<.05[b]	19
Other ear, nose, and throat diagnoses	<.001[a]	18
ACS, dehydration, volume depletion	<.05[a]	18
Cellulitis	<.01[a]	18
410 Chemotherapy	<.01[a]	18
Chemotherapy/radiotherapy	<.05[a]	18
Depressive neurosis	<.01[a]	14

Note: MDC= Major Diagnostic Category;
             ACS = Ambulatory Care Sensitive
[a] Above state average.
[b] Below state average.

Source: Codman Research Group. [2]

the primary care system should mount programs directed at changing dietary behavior. Focus groups are needed to supplement or substitute for communitywide surveys. Surveys cannot reach the illiterate, and response rates may be poor for many other groups. Focus groups are not regarded as being completely representative of the community from which they are drawn, but they have the advantage of being a richer source of qualitative impressions and values than surveys, especially when those surveys are in the form of market research conducted by competing health care corporations.

6. *Physician office billing systems.* Most people who reside in a community will visit a local physician at least once in a two- or three-year period. The physician's bill will show the health problems addressed. Therefore, morbidity patterns can be computed from office billing systems, if their owners will share them. And, of course, HMO databases will include all of this information.

All six of the data sources described above can be used to estimate morbidity patterns for a community. The costs and accuracy of each are different, and ideally all six would be used to describe the health of the community.

Once the magnitude of health problems in the community has been estimated, the governing board must set priorities. Not all health problems are equally important. For example, services for children may outweigh mental health services, according to the local value system. Whether or not the managers of the health system agree, children's health care must come first under these circumstances. Otherwise, community support could well be withdrawn from a health care delivery system perceived as unresponsive.

Community values can be determined by giving consumers as many opportunities as possible to provide input. Focus groups, surveys, town meetings, and inclusion of consumers on the governing board are all useful. The instincts of community leaders are generally consistent with local values.

Priority health problems readily suggest priority health services. Once priorities are established, it will be necessary to compare priorities with the actual array of services available. An inventory of services available is needed. For example, the distance to each of a variety of health services could be displayed in a chart like that shown in Figure 3.1. This approach does not allow planners to compare the volume of each type of service

Service	Availability			
	Local	Town A	Town B	Within 100 Miles
Primary medical care				
Hospital care				
Tertiary care				
Specialty care				
Long-term care				
Emergency care				
Pharmacy				
Dentistry				
Home health care				
Other home care				
Mental health care				
Hospice				
Substance abuse treatment				
Community health nursing				
Health education/wellness ctr.				
Other				
Other				
Other				

FIGURE 3.1. Sample inventory form listing availability of services. An X in the appropriate box(es) indicates where each service can be found.

with the volume needed. However, no standard volume measures are available for common community-based services such as sexually transmitted disease counseling, substance abuse treatment visits, and hospice care for terminally ill patients.[3] Hopefully, these can be developed at some time in the near future.

In addition to examining proximity to various services, planners generally evaluate production capacity for key services. Physician services serve to illustrate the point. Table 3.4 shows what the American Medical Association (AMA) regards as the minimum number of full-time equivalent (FTE) physicians per 1000 clients.[4]

The key primary care provider in most locations is the family practitioner or general practitioner (.432 needed per 1000). Other specialties sometimes included in primary care are general internal medicine, general pediatrics, and obstetrics/gynecology.

Table 3.4—Full-Time Equivalent (FTE) Physicians Needed per 1000 Population in an Aggressively Managed System (55% Commercial and 45% Seniors)

Specialty	Targeted FTEs/1000
General family practice	0.432
General internal medicine	0.086
Other internal medicine	0.399
Pediatrics	0.143
Obstetrics/gynecology	0.104
Psychiatry	0.048
Cardiovascular	0.060
Ear, nose, and throat	0.075
Ophthalmology	0.020
General surgery	0.101
Orthopedic surgery	0.119
Urological surgery	0.037
Other surgery	0.048
Emergency medicine	0.020
Radiology	0.047
Pathology	0.087
Anesthesiology	0.085
Other miscellaneous	0.055
Total	**1.966**

Source: American Medical Association. [4]

The total number of physicians needed comes out to about 2 per 1000 population.

In some communities, the governing board may value access to specialists more highly than these rates allow. The board may choose to increase the number of FTE specialists and reduce the number of family practitioners. Or it may choose to supplement primary care physicians with midlevel providers. Regardless of the final plan, the point remains that the mix and availability of providers should be consciously planned, taking into account local values as well as benchmarks provided by national organizations such as the AMA.

A similar approach can be used to plan for acute care hospital beds. Often, planners assume that 2 community hospital beds are needed per 1000 clients. Posthospital convalescent care and long-term nursing home care could occur in the same facility if more than 2 beds per 1000 were available locally. Bed-to-population ratios for inpatient mental health, substance abuse treatment, and other specialized services can be based on local priorities. Numbers of FTEs devoted to services not requiring inpatient beds are also a matter for local priorities to determine. For example, community health nursing is an essential component of a primary care system. However, the degree to which community health nurses can spearhead outreach programs and health education and the degree to which they will be able to seek out vulnerable populations such as migrant laborers, undocumented aliens, or the elderly will depend on local needs and priorities. No absolute correct number of nurses per 1000 can be offered, just as there is no correct number of family practitioners per 1000.

The above discussion assumes that the health system is serving a defined community. In most situations, the community will be a market area consisting of a known population residing in geographic proximity. While many methods have been used to estimate service areas, the most reasonable is to allocate zip codes or townships to a community if the plurality of residents use primary care providers in that community. This allows compiling of micro areas to form a denominator for population-based planning.

Forecasting Demand in an Era of Managed Care

For planners, more information is always desirable. In planning for hospital care, the following would be ideal: (1) a complete listing of all current and future situations requiring care in the subject population; (2) accurate estimates of the amounts of resources required to meet those needs; and (3) complete knowledge of the resources available and their capacities to provide services.

Planning for primary care also has sometimes attempted to meet this ideal. Usually, however, planners do not have information available about the prevalence and stages of all relevant types of morbidity in small areas. Suffice it to say at this point that planners should regard themselves as fortunate if they possess only number 3 above.

Given a lack of knowledge about the prevalence of situations requiring hospital care, how can planners estimate current and future requirements? The first step is to forecast utilization and the second step is to convert the utilization forecasts into resources such as beds and personnel. We discuss forecasting in this section.

Three forecasting methods are employed by planners: demand models, historical demand, and norms. Demand models are multivariate equations composed of predictors of demand for care, with demand measured by utilization rates. Included in the models are factors such as income, insurance coverage, distance to the treatment site from the consumer's home or office, the number of relevant health professionals in the area, the attractiveness of the provider organization, the quality of clinical resources (e.g., physician hours, hospital patient days) available for use, and such measures of population health status as are available. These equations are estimated with data for many market areas, then offered to local planners who seek to forecast future service volume. The results should be accurate from the perspective of economic theory, but they rarely are.

The best predictors of future use rates in a particular area are recent past use rates in that area, adjusted for demographic changes. The main disadvantage of using the historical utilization rate is that the method assumes that medical practice has been reasonably appropriate, and thus tends to reinforce the status quo. If an area has always had 150 discharges per 1000 population, then it will continue to have that many if physicians are given license to admit as they choose and hospital administrators are given sufficient resources to provide that level of service.

An alternative approach is to use normative use rates to forecast need for care, with the understanding that need for care may be different from demand. Public health planners will have an understandable preference for need, because the difference between need and demand often lies in wealth. After all, by definition demand is the amount of services people will consume at a given price. Corollary to this is the observation that a shortage can always be eliminated, in an economist's mind, by raising the price. Need cannot be gotten rid of so easily.

Normative use rates are a valid and workable approach to health planning. For example, let us assume that a given community has about 130 hospital discharges per 1000 population. A comparison with the discharge rates shown in Table 3.5 suggests that excess hospitalization is occurring in the area.[5] The planner might use this information by forecasting a need for hospital services that is much lower than historical use rates would indicate.

However, the planner may have been misled in reaching this conclusion. The rates shown in Table 3.5 have been adjusted for age, whereas the actual utilization rate for our hypothetical community (130 per 1000) may not have been. (Note: an excellent discussion of methods for adjustment of rates is presented in Dever.[6]) To be valid, normative use rates must be adjusted for differences in population characteristics. Then the forecasts they generate must be converted into resource requirements. These topics are be addressed in the next two sections of this chapter.

As indicated above, the number of people requiring hospitalization in a given population is rarely known. The incidence rates of some diseases are reported for small areas in the *Morbidity and Mortality Weekly Report* published by the Centers for Disease Control and Prevention, and in some areas planners have managed to accumulate data about the prevalence of certain chronic diseases. Unfortunately, it is difficult to know what proportion of people with these conditions will require

Table 3.5—Discharge Rates (Adjusted for Age), Non-Federal Short-Stay Hospitals, 1993

	Discharges per 1000 Population
Northeast	81.7
Midwest	98.4
South	96.2
West	69.9
United States	88.1

Source: National Center for Health Statistics. [5]

hospitalization. Furthermore, no data source has complete prevalence information on all conditions that might require hospital services.

Planners may choose to conduct special surveys to catalog illness or apply sophisticated measures of population health status. Quality of life surveys might detect unmet needs of a variety of patient groups, but such surveys are very costly. Furthermore, normative service utilization rates are not available for detailed breakdowns. As a result, planners usually fall back on basic census categories such as age, sex, and race as proxies for health status.

The planner should remember that some hospital services are consumed primarily by special populations. For example, obstetrical admissions are disproportionately composed of women between the ages of 15 and 44. Therefore, obstetrical use rates should be constructed not with total population as the denominator, but with the number of women in the relevant age group. Similarly, pediatric and geriatric unit admissions should be forecast separately.

Since forecasts cannot be made for admissions for each specific diagnosis, it is useful to make the forecast for all hospital admissions experienced by the subject population, then apportion part of them to each diagnostic category according to their historical proportions. Similarly, forecasts should be made for the entire region served and admissions apportioned to each hospital according to expected market share. This procedure gives the planner the option of using a normatively derived market share or adjusting market share to reflect expected changes. For example, if one of the hospitals serving an area is expected to open a new, ultramodern facility, then its market share might be expected to increase and those of its competitors to decrease.

Estimating Resource Requirements: The Hospital Example

Inpatient hospital services have received the attention of public health planners perhaps more than any other personal health services. There are several reasons for this. First, the cost of investment in new hospital plant is high, requiring either public funds or loans. Since return on investment is low for investor-owned hospitals and (theoretically) nonexistent for not-for-profits, capital has tended to be scarce. From 1946 to the 1970s, the federal government provided investment subsidies via the Hill-Burton program. Naturally, federal administrators asked the states to develop plans so that they could be sure the Hill-Burton funds were being invested wisely. Today, managed care is forcing hospitals to rethink their bed requirements because hospital admissions and days of care are less likely to be reimbursed than was true in previous decades.

A second reason why planners have tended to concentrate on inpatient hospital services is because of a suspicion that excess investment in hospital services leads to overutilization. The famous Roemer's Law ("A bed built is a bed filled") was treated with distrust by American health economists, but not by those in Europe, where most consumers faced no price constraints because of public financing. In fact, the notion that demand would be less than infinite seemed naive in those circumstances.

Third, hospital expenditures constitute the largest line item on the national bill of health expenditures. Therefore, planners in an era of cost containment must try to find some trimmable fat.

Fourth, data on hospital use are more readily available than information on other types of personal health services. Planning is data-driven, and plans are more likely to be made in areas for which supporting data can be presented.

Finally, planners have tried to reduce expenditures for hospital services by substituting ambulatory care for inpatient care. Touted by reformers as "community based" and a strategy for empowering consumers by preventing institutionalization, ambulatory care also had the advantage (to insurance companies and employers) of being paid for out of consumers' pockets. Even though the total social cost of convalescence outside the hospital might be greater because of foregone economies of scale, most of that cost is absorbed by families who must take time off work to help the sick person and who also usually pay higher copayments for such convalescent care than they do for inpatient care. But these costs tend to be ignored because they are not borne by third-party payers.

In short, hospital planning has received the attention of public health planners because it is important to the public interest. And it should be important to hospital-based planners for the same reason. However, the question remains: How can requirements for hospital services, and other types of services, be estimated? At present no one best way to organize health systems is known, and indeed, our ability to measure improvements in health system performance can be questioned.

All is not lost, however. Some techniques for population-based planning are available, and they are surprisingly simple to apply at either the institutional or the systems level. The purpose of this chapter is to give the reader a working knowledge of these methods. Thus armed with rules of thumb, the managers assisting health planning efforts can discretely scrutinize the plans submitted by self-interested consultants, ivory tower academics, and growth-oriented health care administrators and clinicians with some confidence that gross distortions can be detected. The techniques discussed here can be applied to both hospital and nonhospital services.

Imagine that a small rural hospital in Iowa is in financial distress and is seeking state aid to help maintain its operations. You have the following information about the hospital:

$$\text{Past Occupancy} = \text{ADC}/\text{Beds} = 0.50$$
$$\text{ALOS} = \text{Patient Days}/\text{Discharges} = 7$$
$$\text{Beds} = 50$$
$$\text{Patient Days} = 9125$$
$$\text{ADC} = \text{Occupancy} \bullet \text{Beds} = 25$$
$$= \text{Patient Days}/365 = 25$$
$$\text{ADC} \bullet \text{Discharges} = \text{Patient Days}$$
$$\text{ADC}/\text{Occupancy Rate} = \text{Beds}$$
$$\text{Patient Days}/\text{ALOS} = \text{Discharges}$$

where ADC is average daily census and ALOS is average length of stay. You also know that an occupancy rate of 0.60 should be achievable for hospitals of this type. The following formula computes the number of beds required:

Beds Needed = [(Discharges • ALOS)/365] / Occupancy
             = (patient days/365)/Occupancy
             = ADC/Occupancy
             = 25 / 0.6
             = 41.7.

The reader may wonder where the normative occupancy rate was obtained. First, note that occupancy rates have been declining nationally for almost a generation because of changes in the practice of medicine and in reimbursement procedures. Therefore, the nation as a whole is overbedded, and average occupancy does not provide an adequate standard. In situations such as these, the planner must rely on the judgment of knowledgeable informants, including advisory committees and consultants.

The above example introduces the general approach, but it is not complete in itself. The following refinements should be considered: estimating requirements for particular types of services rather than for the entire hospital; using a normative forecast; adopting a normative ALOS; adjusting for the effect of case mix on ALOS; estimating requirements for personnel rather than beds.

Continuing with the above example, assume that the hospital is the sole provider in a community of 10 000 residents. The discharge rate per 1000 population is (9125/ALOS)/10 000 = 0.13 • 1000 = 130. However, you know that a discharge rate of 90 per 1000 is reasonable for this community. Therefore, a reasonable forecast of needed hospital admissions is (90/1000) • 10 000 = 900. Using equation 1 above, you can now estimate the number of hospital beds required to be [(900 • 7)/365] / 0.6 = 28.8.

Suppose, however, that you know ALOS for hospitals of this type can be 6 days instead of 7. Bed requirements change as follows: [(900 • 6)/365] / 0.6 = 24.7.

ALOS norms can be obtained from American Hospital Association statistics published annually. Tables 3.6 and 3.7, for example, show computation of ALOS for hospitals of different sizes.[7,8] Table 3.6 is limited to acute days but is not specific to Iowa. Table 3.7 is specific to Iowa but does not exclude days in subacute units. If the planner is estimating requirements for acute care beds only, then Table 3.6 is a better source of norms.

However, political realities often force planners to use norms that err on the side of liberality; hence the selection of an ALOS of 6 in this example.

None of these examples includes adjustments for case mix. One might argue that admissions should be forecast separately for each diagnostic category, but this procedure adds no precision to the forecast total because the population at risk for admission in each diagnosis is not known. Instead, it is reasonable to assume that some specific proportion of total admissions will be in each diagnostic category; this assumption yields an expected

Table 3.6—Utilization of Hospital Units Operated by Non-Federal, Short-Stay Community Hospitals, United States, 1993

| | No. of Beds | | | |
	6–24	25–49	50–99	100–199
Admissions	387.8	954.9	1,886.0	4,433.0
Average daily census	5.9	15.6	38.2	83.9
Inpatient days	2,113.1	5,680.1	13,946.4	30,602.2
Average length of stay, days	5.4	5.9	7.4	6.9

Source: Computed from American Hospital Association statistics.[7]

Table 3.7—Utilization of Non-Federal, Short-Stay Community Hospitals, Iowa, 1993

| | No. of Beds | | | |
	6–24	25–49	50–99	100–199
Admissions	350.0	828.1	1206.2	2,584.0
Average daily census	6.1	14.9	33.9	130.6
Inpatient days	2,171.6	5,460.2	12,397.3	30,696.8
Average length of stay, days	6.2	6.6	10.3	11.9

Source: Computed from American Hospital Association Statistics.[8]

number of cases which can then be used to adjust the number of patient days forecast. Examine the following example:

Case Type	Percentage of Discharges	Discharges	ALOS	Days
1	11	100	4	400
2	67	600	5	3000
3	22	200	6	1200
Total		900		4600

Assuming only three case types and certain percentages in each case type, the number of discharges for each can be calculated. ALOS can be taken from the hospital's own history or normative figures can be used. ALOS times discharges yields patient days. The sum of patient days divided by total discharges (4600/900) equals a case mix–adjusted ALOS of 5.1. When the new ALOS is used in the bed requirement calculation, the equation appears as follows:

$$[(900 \bullet 5.1) / 365] / 0.6 = 21 \text{ beds.}$$

Of course, there are hundreds of diagnostic categories and several levels of severity within each, making the computation of case mix–adjusted ALOS a job for a skilled programmer. Alternatively, the planner might assume that the proportion of cases in each case type will remain unchanged, thus permitting use of historical ALOS in a hospital of acceptable efficiency. But if patient turnover may have been slower than necessary, normative adjustment of ALOS is required.

In this example, normative ALOS and occupancy rates have been derived from operating statistics that are broken down by geographic area and bed size. The planner must determine which hospital characteristics cause legitimate differences in performance. Small size is accepted as a legitimate cause of lower occupancy because random fluctuations in patient demand have a more dramatic impact on a small facility. Region, on the other hand, is a legitimate adjustment only if there are unmeasured factors that cause regional differences, a dubious point but one that local boards often find plausible.

Hospital performance may also vary by ownership (investor-owned, not-for-profit, government), affiliation (system or nonsystem), location (urban or rural), service mix, teaching status, medical staff organization (salaried, closed staff, open staff), and volume of surgical activity. Normative occupancy rates, ALOS, and input costs could be found for most types of hospitals by searching the health services research literature. However, this begs the question of whether or not to adjust for known performance differences among hospital types. The planner could take the position that the public interest demands the most efficient hospital system possible and therefore no adjustment should be made if a particular hospital is of a type that has lower occupancy rates or longer stays. According to this position, the occupancy rates and ALOS achieved by the most efficient types of hospitals should be the norms.

Taking a dogmatic stance on this point will embroil the planner in controversy, since many provider organizations will regard this as an inequitable position. After all, rural managers cannot relocate their hospitals to urban areas and thus overcome the diseconomies of small scale and geographically dispersed patients.

A wiser course is to use averages as norms, rather than extremes such as the most efficient hospital that can be found. This strategy incrementally moves the hospital system toward greater efficiency without calling for massive dislocations. It also prevents the planner from making major errors, always a possibility when plans are based on imperfect data and incomplete science.

In the past, public health planners have been criticized for placing an undue emphasis on hospital bed supply. In an age of prospective reimbursement, low occupancy rates may be irrelevant; after all, Medicare will not pay a hospital more simply for being inefficient. Hospital administrators know that they should not staff empty beds. On the other hand, they may not wish to close them, because it may prove impossible to gain approval to reopen them later. Even so, market forces are vastly changing bed supply across America. For example, 16 hospitals closed in the Chicago area between 1984 and 1996, with perhaps 17 left in distress.

For this reason, the planner may be well advised to forecast the average daily census rather than estimating bed requirements. The expected census is an indication of the volume of inpatient activity and can lead to discussions about the

Table 3.8—Computation of Staffing Ratio for Non-Federal, Short-Stay Community Hospitals, Iowa, 1993

	No. of Beds			
	6–24	25–49	50–99	100–199
Average daily census	6.1	14.9	33.9	130.6
Personnel	54.9	101.6	160.6	353.4
Patients/FTEE	.11	.15	.21	.37
Staff/patient	9.0	6.8	4.7	2.7

Source: Computed from American Hospital Association Statistics.[8]
Note: FTEE=Full-time equivalent employee.

relationship between the acute care mission and the needs of the community. Since forecasting can be highly uncertain, a sensitivity analysis should be employed to determine the impact of various assumptions on the forecast. In the example below, census is shown to vary according to the size of the market area and the market share.

Market Share	Small Service Area[a]	Large Service Area[b]
.10	1.4	3.9
.25	3.5	9.7
.50	7.0	19.5
.75	10.4	29.2

[a] Year 2000 population = 6343, discharges/1000 = 100, ALOS = 8 days, ADC = 13.9 for area.

[b] Year 2000 population = 17 736, discharges/1000 = 100, ALOS = 8 days, ADC = 38.9 for area.

Even the average daily census may be relatively unimportant in a highly diversified small hospital. What, then, is the key input that planners should control? The answer might well be personnel. The bed sizing equation can be converted into a full-time equivalent employee (FTEE) model as follows:

FTEE needed = [(discharges • ALOS)/365] / (patients/FTEE)
= ADC/(patients/FTEE).

Continuing here with the example of a small hospital in Iowa and assuming that case mix is about the same for all Iowa hospitals of the same size, then a reasonable staffing ratio for our small rural hospital is 0.22 (see Table 3.8).[8] The calculation is then as follows: [(900 • 5.1)/365] / 0.22 = 57 FTEEs needed for the acute care mission.

Government regulators do not control the number of FTEEs, since hospitals are not assigned authorized numbers of FTEEs under certificate-of-need programs, as they are beds. Nevertheless, state planners can use information about labor productivity to evaluate requests for expansion or financial assistance. In some cases, reassignment of acute care staff to other functions may be indicated. And planners are free to address the staffing issue, within the constraints of local politics.

Defining the Service Population

Definition of a service population is important because it permits calculation of use rates, which are essential for forecasting and evaluating system performance. However, service populations are defined in a variety of ways. Using different methods to define service areas will lead to different population estimates, which in turn will bias use rates. The direction and degree of bias are related to residents' tendencies to migrate out of their service areas for hospital care.

For the purpose of forecasting future hospital use, current hospital utilization is expressed in relation to the population served. When a managed care organization has achieved a local monopoly, the list of enrollees is the population served. However, most markets are still a mixture of fee-for-service and capitation, with reimbursement coming from a variety of insurance companies. Under these circumstances, the planner for the local health system is forced to estimate the service population.

Estimation of the service population can be approached in two ways: by first defining a geographic service area or by inference from market share.[9] The latter procedure consists of three steps: (1) estimate for each local area the proportion of its cases treated in each hospital; (2) for each local area, multiply this proportion by its estimated population; and (3) add these numbers for all local areas to obtain an estimate of the total population served by a particular hospital.[10]

Definition of a geographic service area has several advantages over the market share method. When a hospital has assumed responsibility for a geographic area, travel distance can be readily examined and the particular needs of the population can be identified. Furthermore, geographic areas can be compared in terms of quantities of services delivered and the supply of service-producing units available. Therefore, the concept of the service area is especially useful for planning from a broad social perspective. Once the area is defined, it can be characterized by the level of service utilization or the accessibility of services. Evaluation of the performance of the health care system is facilitated.

Public health planners usually construct hospital service areas to be mutually exclusive. Two approaches have been used to develop mutually exclusive service areas.[9,11] A normative approach starts with the notion that there are certain desirable patterns of service use. The planning process can be used to make the health system conform to these normative patterns. For example, it may be seen as a public policy goal to have a regionalized hospital system with dispersed clinics feeding admissions to secondary care centers, which, in turn, refer complex cases to tertiary care centers. In this kind of controlled health care system, it is natural to assign service areas to particular hospitals and hold the hospitals accountable for the quantity and effectiveness of services delivered.

The use of normative service areas to implement regionalization is risky, since investments will be wasted if patients go elsewhere. However, normative areas can be used for another purpose—strategic planning. A hospital might define a geographic area as a service target, with forecasts based on the assumption that the target area will be serviced.

Hospital service areas can also be constructed empirically. A service area can be defined as a collection of counties (or townships, zip codes, or census tracts) in which the residents rarely leave the area for hospital care. If more than one hospital is within the area, then the hospitals are regarded as constituting a cluster. Patient origin and destination data (hereafter called patient origin data) are usually used to define service areas in epidemiological studies of health care utilization.

Table 3.9—Patient Origin and Destination Data: Discharges (and Market Share) by Hospital and County of Patient's Residence

County	Hospital A	B	C	Other	Total No. of Discharges
West	100	200	300	100	700
	(.14)	(.29)	(.43)	(.14)	
East	75	175	275	75	600
	(.13)	(.29)	(.46)	(.13)	
North	250	150	50	50	500
	(.50)	(.30)	(.10)	(.10)	
South	300	200	100	100	700
	(.43)	(.29)	(.14)	(.14)	
Other	50	50	50	50	200
Total					2,700

Table 3.9 illustrates how patient origin data might be arrayed. The market shares in each county are computed by dividing the hospital's discharges to the county by the total discharges experienced by the county's population. Using a plurality rule to assign counties to service areas leads to the conclusion that West and East are in hospital C's service area and North and South are in hospital A's service area. This leaves hospital B without a service area, clearly an unacceptable result. A simple remedy is to define hospitals A, B, and C as a cluster and all four counties as the cluster's service area.

As this example illustrates, patient origin data are likely to reveal that mutually exclusive service areas do not exist, especially in urban areas and for specialty hospitals. Service areas may overlap and may have different boundaries for different services. Rice and Creel, in a text explaining hospital forecasting methods, offered three options for defining the service areas of a hospital: (1) using the geographic area that is the source of 80% to 85% of the hospital's admissions; (2) including any small area that contributes at least 10% of the hospital's admissions; and (3) including any small area in which the hospital has at least a 10% market share.[12] When used to construct individualized service areas for every hospital in a community, all three of these options result in overlapping, rather than mutually exclusive, service areas.

Garnick et al. identified two additional methods for identifying market areas which are shared by several hospitals.[13] In the first, a convenient geopolitical boundary is selected. For example, all hospitals in a Standard Metropolitan Statistical Area might be considered to be in the same service area. In the second method, distances between hospitals are used to define market areas. Garnick et al. used a 15-mile radius to define a set of competing hospitals. Actually, as they pointed out, both the distance method and the geopolitical boundary method identify areas of potential rather than actual competition.

The overlapping service area methods share a common characteristic with the mutually exclusive service area methods: they relate the utilization of a hospital (or cluster of hospitals) to the population of a geographic area, even though all of the patients treated in the hospital may not be from the service area and not all of the patients from the service area use the hospital. Therefore, forecasts based on the population of a service area all have a built-in bias. It is possible to avoid errors arising from migration, however, by forecasting utilization for the entire service population regardless of the source of care. Then the forecast for the individual hospital is derived by multiplying its market share times total use.

Regionalization

Many planners assume that the health system should be made more rational, meaning that duplication of resources should be eliminated and the savings reallocated to fill gaps in the array of needed resources. For example, some hospital resources might be reallocated to primary care.

The vehicle for imposing rationality on the health system is the concept of regionalization, which was discussed in chapter 2. Regionalization is assumed to be better than an unfettered competitive market for health services for several reasons. First, competition has been shown to have less benefit than its proponents claim. Second, there are several costs regionalization may reduce. These include both production and transaction costs. Production costs are reduced in a regionalized system because having fewer, larger hospitals (rather than several competing hospitals) permits achievement of economies of scale and scope. Transaction costs are incurred when the hospital must purchase materials and services from a market and when clients must shop for hospital care. Vertical integration, whereby the hospital and its suppliers (e.g., doctors) are part of a single system, and horizontal integration, where hospitals are cooperative parts of a system rather than competitors, can reduce transaction costs. Both types of integration occur in regionalization.

Third, regionalization may reduce the inefficiencies and poor quality that can occur when complex procedures are performed infrequently. This is why some experts will propose that only one hospital in a region be allowed to perform certain procedures, such as open-heart surgery. The designated hospital will be able to maintain higher volume and, it is hoped, better outcomes than competing hospitals would be able to do.

Fourth, regionalization avoids the destructive effects of competition. When forced to compete, hospitals and doctors may engage in misleading advertising. Advertising costs themselves may be regarded as wasteful when they go beyond providing public information and health education. Competitors may also spend more on consumer luxuries such as amenities and longer hospital stays in an effort to lure patients away from other providers. Furthermore, hospitals are less able to provide essential but unprofitable services when competition reduces excess revenue.

Finally, regionalization eliminates excess hospital capacity, thus reducing the potential for unnecessary admissions. Since a hospital admission is more costly than outpatient care, elimination of unnecessary admissions is vital to operation of an efficient health system.

A reasonable outline of a regionalized system would have the following features:[14]

- Comprehensive primary care would be provided by organized group practices serving 10 000 to 30 000 people.
- Community hospital care (secondary care) would serve four or five primary care populations. These hospitals would provide two or three beds per 1000 population served. Outpatient,

specialty, maternity, limited surgery, short-term mental illness, detoxification, emergency, and extended care (e.g., nursing homes, halfway houses, and residential care facilities) services would be offered.
- Regional (tertiary care) hospitals, offering about one hospital bed per 1000 population, would serve about 10 community care hospitals. Some tertiary care medical centers would be university hospitals serving three to five regional hospitals—areas comprising 1.5 to 2.5 million people.

This outline is only that; it is not and cannot be a detailed blueprint, accurately describing the quantities of hospital resources needed in all area. As an outline, however, it can offer benchmarks local and regional planning bodies and managers of health care delivery organizations can use to guide investment decisions. Working out the details will require more information about local needs.

Planning for Ambulatory Medical Care

As the spread of managed care has constrained the use of inpatient care, nonhospital services have become as important as hospital care. Furthermore, the needs of the chronically ill—many of which are for outpatient services—increasingly demand more of the attention of planners and policymakers. Therefore, planning for nonhospital care is rapidly becoming more important than planning for hospital services.

The art of planning for office visits to physicians is not well developed. At present, one complex and two simple approaches can be offered for estimating requirements for ambulatory medical care in a particular geographic area. The complex method was developed by Lee and Jones (cited in Donabedian[9]) as part of the studies conducted by the Committee on the Costs of Medical Care in 1929. The Lee and Jones method entailed the following steps:

1. *Classification of diseases.* Lee and Jones used 19 categories.
2. *Age-specific estimates of disease prevalence.* Lee and Jones had to rely on professional judgments.

3. *Standards of service.* Estimates of services required for the treatment of the disease categories were obtained from "leading practitioners." A conservative style was emphasized; luxury services were omitted. Standards were detailed as to physician specialty, type of visit, number of visits, and minutes per visit, thus permitting computation of total service hours per case. Nonphysician personnel requirements and diagnostic procedure rates were also estimated.

4. *Productivity norms.* For example, physicians were assumed to provide 2000 hours of work per year.

5. *Computations.* Number 2 above can be multiplied by the standards from 3, then divided by the productivity norms in 4 to yield the number of personnel required.

The Lee and Jones method, while logical in the extreme, suffers from three major weaknesses. First, professional judgments of service requirements may be criticized as subject to recall bias. In addition, they tend to reinforce past practice. Second, productivity is likely to be influenced by the way that medical care is organized, as well as a host of other factors. Third, acceptable and current estimates of service requirements and acceptable and current productivity norms are not available to planners. Therefore, the planner must rely on other methods.

Both of the simpler approaches to estimating requirements use population ratios. The first, the visit rate method, applies a normative number of visits per unit of population to a population forecast or estimate. The second, the provider rate method, applies a normative number of providers per unit of population to a population forecast or estimate.

Norms can be derived from a variety of sources. Use of local rates requires the least disruption in patterns of care but has the effect of preserving the inefficiencies inherent in the status quo. Rates achieved by laudably efficient systems, such as some HMOs, can also serve as norms. While it is known that HMOs can provide care to more people with fewer physicians, the implications of this information are unclear. Perhaps the planner should assume that HMO use rates and levels of productivity can be used as standards in any geographic area. On the other hand, it may be more reasonable to assume that practice style cannot be influenced by the planner in the short run. A compromise approach is to use national rates.

Table 3.10—Physician Office Visits per Person per Year			
Office Visits to Ambulatory Care Physicians[a]		Physician Contacts in Office[b]	
Males			
Age	Rate	Age	Rate
0–14	2.30	0–17	2.5
15–24	1.33	18–44	1.9
25–44	1.64	45–64	3.2
45–64	2.61	64+	4.9
64+	4.61		
Females			
0–14	2.32	0–17	2.5
15–24	2.53	18–44	3.3
25–44	3.24	45–64	3.7
45–64	3.55	64+	5.3
64+	5.01		

[a] Rates are for 1985. Data from the National Center for Health Statistics.[15 (Table 1)]

[b] Rates are for 1987. Data from the National Center for Health Statistics.[16]

Norms available for use in estimating physician requirements are shown in Tables 3.10 and 3.11.[15–17] Table 3.10 lists office visit rates per person per year. These rates can be multiplied by projected population to forecast the number of visits needed in a community. Visits may be 15 to 20 minutes in length on average. Total office visit time in hours would then be equal to forecast number of visits times 0.25 (one fourth of an hour) or 0.33 (one third of an hour). Computation of the number of physicians required becomes possible if the number of hours a typical physician spends in office practice is known (total visit hours divided by hours available per physician). Unfortunately, no reasonable norms can be offered for physician office hours that would be valid for small areas. The actual number of hours available in a particular community would depend on the number of hours local doctors are willing to work and the degree to which local physicians provide care to nonresidents. If some clients travel to the community for specialty care or hospital services, then local physicians will spend proportionately less time in office practice treating local clients. Therefore, norms for the number of hours available for office visits provided to community residents must be developed by informed judgments of local experts or by special surveys. The practicality of the visit rate method for estimating requirements for office care founders on this point.

The physician population ratio method attempts to avoid this issue by using normative rates of physicians per person to estimate requirements in any particular small area. Examples of normative rates are shown in Table 3.11. The number of physicians available can be seen to vary widely between urban and rural areas and by state. One obvious reason for this variation is physicians' preference for some areas over others. In addition, a larger number of physicians may be attracted to an area because more are needed. A community may need more physicians per person if a local physician is semiretired or if nonresidents travel to the community for care.

In short, selection of an appropriate norm for a small area is problematic. The problem can be minimized, however, by

Table 3.11—Physicians per 100,000 Population, 1985	
US	
HMOs	120.0
Urban counties	174.7
Rural counties	53.0
Total	164.8
Small rural counties	
Georgia	31.3
California	86.2
Iowa	53.3
Total	40.8
Primary care	
Metro counties	75.5
Nonmetro counties	53.9
HMOs	57.6
US Total	70.4
Source: Data from Kindig and Movassaghi.[17]	

planning for medium-sized areas (such as counties) rather than very small areas (such as zip codes or townships). This procedure minimizes the impact of the additional workload required by incoming nonresidents. Furthermore, norms are more likely to be valid on average for medium-sized areas; under- or overestimates for the very small areas within the county will tend to cancel each other out. And patients living on the borders of very small areas can easily reallocate themselves to physicians who can handle the additional patient load.

In the above discussion, three important issues were not taken into account: the selection of physician rate norms, planning for nonphysician personnel, and the content of office practice. These concerns are interrelated. An HMO rate of primary care physicians per person could be selected as the norm. However, this procedure assumes that the use of support personnel will be similar to that found in the more responsible HMOs. In addition, it assumes that physicians in the area being planned for will practice with a primary care orientation, meaning that they will seek to coordinate all of the needs of their patients rather than just treating the current set of symptoms.

A primary care approach to medical office practice may be desirable, but it cannot be imposed by the planner. Therefore, the following recommendations are made:

- The planner should work toward development of a prepaid group practice form of medical care organization. In the meantime, however, national rates should be used as norms. This has the effect of increasing the supply of primary care providers in shortage areas and reducing it in surplus areas even though the ideal number of physicians and other personnel per 1000 people is unknown.
- The number of nurses and support personnel required will depend upon the local balance of physicians and other primary care personnel. The planner may be well advised to let the market determine the supply of nonphysician staff in local areas. Alternatively, a reasonable ratio of physicians to nonphysicians may be assumed. For example, a one-to-one ratio of physicians to nurse practitioners would allow for cost-effective team practice. (Note: The number of nurses and other health professionals required has been estimated for the nation by means of a demand model. See *Health Personnel in the United States*[18] for details. This type of

model is not useful at the local level unless the planner assumes that personnel will play the same roles they are assumed to play in the national forecasting model.)

Planning for Mental Health and Substance Abuse Services

This section addresses planning for outpatient behavioral health services only. Needs for inpatient mental health care can be estimated in the same fashion as that described for hospital planning. Indeed, most inpatient psychiatric care is provided in community hospitals; thus, estimated bed and staff requirements for those hospitals would include psychiatric care.[19] The reader should note, however, that insurance companies are reluctant to pay for inpatient care. Therefore, planning for ambulatory services is far more critical at this point in history.

The prevalence of psychiatric disorders in the general population has been studied extensively. As a result, we now know about how many people might be expected to have a variety of diagnoses in a typical community. The number of outpatient visits persons with each diagnosis are likely to make is also known. However, these two kinds of rates are not immediately useful for planning, for two reasons. First, the actual prevalence of mental illness is not known for small areas unless a special survey is performed. Prevalence may be estimated from demographic characteristics, but the planner may as well estimate service use directly from demographics and thus avoid dealing with rough estimates of prevalence. Second, the utilization rates for people with particular disorders may not be valid for the small area for which plans are being made. Once again, we are led to the conclusion that utilization rates should be applied directly to the population in demographic categories, leaving prevalence out of the equation. Thirdly, the diagnosis of mental illness in population surveys is fraught with difficulties, casting doubt on the accuracy of the rates. And finally, many visits triggered by mental illness are actually made to medical providers rather than to mental health specialists. Therefore, prevalence can give a misleading estimate of the requirements for mental health services.

The first step in estimating requirements for facilities and providers of various types is to estimate the number of people in the community who need care. Then some standards of care can be applied to develop forecasts of the number of units of service required. The expected productivity of providers can be used to convert services into numbers of clinicians. However, lack of data makes this approach difficult to apply.

Needs Assessment

The assessment of need for mental health services for particular geographic areas has long been a methodological challenge. One important aspect of the problem is that the most impaired victims are less likely to seek out services appropriately.[20] Clinically, a distinct difference can be found between those with psychiatric illnesses and those with less severe mental health problems. The seriously mentally ill require medical treatment in consultation with or under the supervision of a psychiatrist. Individuals who have trouble coping, have nonspecific worries and distress, or have less severe forms of depression may not require medical supervision. Estimation of resource requirements will have to take into account these differences in types of services required. As substance abuse treatment becomes integrated into mental health care, an additional layer of complexity is added.

Approaches to needs assessment include the following:

1. *Epidemiological surveys.* Direct assessment of the prevalence of psychiatric disorder in a community is prohibitively expensive, though it offers the most reliable data for planning.

2. *Social indicator analysis.* Indicators thought to be related to need for mental health care include variables such as the following: median income of families, percent of families in poverty, percentage unemployed, percentage employed in low-status occupations, median years of school completed, percentage of population of foreign stock, percentage of persons in group quarters, percentage of teenagers not in school, and percentage of mothers of preschool children in the labor force.[20] Other indicators include rates of juvenile delinquency, divorce, sexually transmitted disease, and child abuse, and percentages of library

card holders and registered voters. The frequency of fire alarms has been proposed as an indicator of the prevalence of mental illness, since fire starting is not rare among hospitalized mental patients.[20] The obvious problem with the social indicator approach is that the selection of indicators is hampered by uncertain correlations with prevalence of mental health problems and the absence of standards for quantities of services required for different levels of the indicators.

3. *Treatment rate analysis.* Availability of services affects treatment rates, as does a tendency to avoid treatment even when it is needed. Further complicating the issue is that the majority of mental health cases are not treated by mental health specialists (see Table 3.14).[21] Therefore, treatment rates are not direct measures of need for care. On the other hand, it makes little sense to plan for the ability to deliver a higher quantity of services than are likely to be used. Furthermore, previous utilization rates may be accurate predictors of future demand for services. Perhaps most useful is the potential to compare utilization rates for different population subgroups for the purpose of identifying groups that receive lower than expected quantities of services.

4. *Surveys of consumers, community leaders, or service providers.* Conceptually simple and relatively inexpensive, community surveys have the advantage of discovering what people in the community value and therefore what services they are likely to use and be willing to pay to support. On the other hand, lay perceptions of need may be highly inaccurate. Professional judgments about care needs may be based more on practice style or professional background than on scientifically validated standards.

5. *Combination approaches.* A multistep approach was described by Rabkin, who suggested using social indicators to rank communities according to need for care.[20] Then communities would be ranked according to the treatment rates. Communities in which need was high but treatment rates were low would be targeted for community surveys.

Of the five options described above, none is ideal. Synthetic estimates of the prevalence of mental illness can be developed by applying prevalence rates developed in large-scale studies to local areas. For example, Table 3.12 shows the prevalence rates aggregated from five sites for the major mental disorders.[21] Multiplying these rates by the population of a community would generate estimates of local prevalence rates. For example, 28.1% of adults might be expected to suffer from a mental health problem. If a county has a population of 10 000 adults, then 2810 would have mental disorders. Of these, 27.8% (781 people) might be expected to receive ambulatory treatment (Table 3.13).[21]

Table 3.12—Ambulatory Mental Health Visits per Person Aged 18 or Older and Prevalence by Disorder, 1990

Disorder	SMA	General Medical	Prevalence, 1 y
Any DIS ADM disorder	15.3	3.9	28.1
Any disorder except alcohol/drug	15.8	4.1	22.1
Comorbid mental and substance use disorder	12.9	3.9	3.3
Any substance use disorder	12.4	3.2	9.5
Alcohol	12.8	2.9	7.4
Drug	12.3	3.6	3.1
Schizophrenia	13.4	3.7	1.1
Any affective disorder	17.3	4.6	9.5
Bipolar I or II	13.9	5.2	1.2
Unipolar major depression	19.4	4.7	5.0
Dysthymia	...	...	5.4
Any anxiety disorder	16.0	4.0	12.6
Phobia	16.0	4.0	10.9
Panic disorder	15.9	6.5	1.3
Obsessive-compulsive disorder	18.3	4.6	2.1
Somatization	20.7	10.4	0.2
Antisocial personality	16.4	3.0	1.5
Severe cognitive impairment	7.9	5.0	2.7
Subthreshold cases	11.8	3.2	...

Source: Bourdon et al.[21] (Table 3.1)

Note: SMA = Specialized mental or addictive service;
DIS ADM = Diagnostic Interview Survey/Alcohol, Drug, and Mental Illness.

Unfortunately, accurate needs assessments probably will reveal high levels of unmet need. For example, only about 64% of persons with schizophrenia receive services in a given year.[21] The percentages are 61 for bipolar disorder, 54 for unipolar major depression, and 45 for obsessive-compulsive disorder. In short, almost half of serious mental illness goes untreated.

Estimating Service Needs

Service requirements per case could be multiplied by estimated prevalence to produce total service requirements for the area. Table 3.12 shows that 15.3 visits are made to specialty mental health providers per person with a disorder. This generates a forecast of 11 949 (15.3 • 781) specialty mental health visits. If this calculation were done for each condition separately, the forecasts could be summed to arrive at visit totals. However, disease-specific forecasts would be determined entirely by the population size of the local area, because the prevalence of each disease is only a synthetic estimate.

Use of aggregated treatment rates has the advantage of not misleading the user of the forecasts about whether true prevalence rates were used in the computations. For example, 5.6% of the adult population used ambulatory mental or addictive services provided by mental health personnel in one year (Table 3.14).[21] Our hypothetical county has 10 000 adult residents, so without knowing diagnoses, we might project 560 clients. If the average client makes 15.3 visits (Table 3.12), then 8568 visits to mental health specialists would be forecast.

A serious limitation inherent in the forecasting methods described above is that they reflect the availability of different types of care at the time the data were collected. Recent changes in the financing of health care have greatly reduced the use of inpatient care and ambulatory care provided by psychiatrists, at least in some markets. Visit rate standards will always reflect certain assumptions about the organization of services and practice standards, yet those assumptions may not hold in the future or in different markets. Therefore, in the absence of some justification for using US averages in 1990 as a reasonable standard for local areas in later time periods, those averages should not be applied blindly.

For example, an analysis of data from the Rand Health Insurance Experiment showed that a generous health insurance plan is likely to stabilize at 6.3 outpatient mental health visits per enrollee a few years after startup. Coinsurance reduces projected utilization to 3.6 visits.[22] In a more recent study, chronically depressed persons were found to use almost 20 psychiatrist visits, 4.3 general medical provider visits, and 17.8 other mental health specialist visits in six months when enrolled in a fee-for-service plan. However, when enrolled in a prepaid plan, utilization dropped to 12.4 psychiatrist visits, 4.5 general medicine provider visits, and 12.6 other mental health specialist visits.[23] This finding confirms variations in the intensity of psychiatric

Table 3.13—Percentages of Persons Aged 18 or Older with a Specific Mental or Addictive Disorder Treated in Inpatient and Ambulatory Service Sectors in One Year

Disorder	Inpatient	Ambulatory	Combined
All persons	0.9	14.5	14.7
Any disorder	2.5	27.8	28.5
Any disorder except alcohol/drug	2.9	31.0	31.9
Comorbid mental and substance use disorder	6.7	36.0	37.4
Any substance use disorder	2.9	22.7	23.6
Alcohol	2.8	21.2	22.0
Drug	3.8	28.1	29.8
Schizophrenia	16.9	59.9	64.3
Any affective disorders	4.7	44.2	45.7
Bipolar I or II	7.6	57.2	60.9
Unipolar major depression	5.8	52.3	53.9
Dysthymia	5.0	40.7	42.1
Any anxiety disorder	3.2	31.7	32.7
Phobia	3.3	30.1	31.1
Panic disorder	8.4	55.4	58.8
Obsessive compulsive disorder	7.4	43.6	45.1
Somatization	10.4	63.2	69.7
Antisocial personality	6.1	28.8	31.1
Severe cognitive impairment	2.9	15.3	17.0
No disorder	0.2	9.1	9.3

Source: Bourdon et al.[21] (Table 3.5)

treatment across markets reported earlier.[24] In the latter study, mean face-to-face minutes ranged from 107 to 360 minutes per patient per month. Adjusting for severity or stage of illness explained much of the variation. However, the treatment philosophy of the clinician also affected intensity. Psychiatric diagnosis was not an important predictor, nor were market factors such as competition among providers and payer mix.

Dependable staff-to-population ratios for staff types other than psychiatrists are not available for mental health services planning, forcing the planner to use the visit rate method. The model employed here to estimate requirements for mental health services and providers is similar to that discussed for other types of services.

1. *Multiply normative admission rates by the size of the population to forecast the number of admissions needed.* In this application, admission refers to initiation of an episode of care, that is, admission to outpatient mental health treatment. The Epidemiological Catchment Area studies found that 5.6%of the population at those sites were likely to visit mental health specialists in one year.[21] Other studies have reported higher rates (see Table 3.15).[21,24-27] Of course, the populations studied may have been underserved, since the quantity of visits demanded is sensitive to price. On the other hand, in the absence of a firm basis for higher estimates the planner should ordinarily be conservative, as we have been in estimating requirements for hospital services.

2. *Multiply the number of admissions by the average number of visits required per client.* Table 3.15 shows differences in visits per case, depending on the survey selected.

3. *Divide the number of visits by the number of visits produced per clinician to calculate the number of personnel required.* The productivity of mental health specialists in terms of numbers of visits will depend on how they function in the local market. For example, some will engage in group sessions—greatly increasing the number of reported visits—while others will work with patients individually. Therefore, a local survey may be required to determine current visit outputs. Alternatively, desired visits per provider can be obtained from model programs. For example, 1350 visits are generated per clinician in the Harvard Community Health Plan.[27]

4. *Use national distributions* (see Table 3.16), *local distributions, and ideal distributions to apportion FTE among provider types.*[21] For example, the Harvard Community Health Plan uses roughly equal proportions of psychiatrists, psychologists, nurses, and therapists.[27]

Long-Term Care Services

Estimating requirements for long-term care services is also fraught with uncertainties. The number of people "requiring" home care, for example, depends on the liberality of the Medicare program. This is not to suggest that needs for home care cannot be objectively determined. On the other hand, people vary in their tolerance for disability, and an individual's desire for help could be greatly affected by the out-of-pocket cost of care. Furthermore, the needs of the chronically disabled can be met with a variety of types of care, including nursing homes, day care, and hospital swing beds as well as home care. Home care may

Table 3.14—Percentages of Adult US Population Using Mental or Addictive Disorder Services in One Year, by Setting

Service	Setting		
	Inpatient	Ambulatory	Combined
Speciality			
mental / addictive	0.9	5.6	5.9
General Medical	0.0	6.4	6.4
Health systems subtotal	0.9	10.7	10.9
Human services	...	3.0	3.0
Professional subtotal	0.9	12.3	12.5
Self-help groups	...	0.7	0.7
Family / friends	...	3.5	3.5
Voluntary support network	...	4.1	4.1
Total	0.9	14.5	14.7

Source: Bourdon et al. [21] (Table 3.2)

Table 3.15—Mental Health Services Utilization Rates, 1990

Survey	% of Population Making a Visit	Visits per Person Making Visits
National Medical Care Utilization and Expenditure Survey[a]	4.3	8.2
National Medical Care Expenditure Survey[b] (Specialist mental health provider visits only	2.0	9.6
Seattle[c]		
Group health	6.4	4.7
Fee-for-service	6.0	17.4
Epidemiological Catchment Area[d]		
Speciality	5.6	14.0
General medical	6.4	3.6
Harvard Community Health Plan[e]	10.0	4.6

Sources: Data from [a] Taube et al.[24]; [b] Horgan.[25]; [c] Wells et al.[26]; [d] Bourdon et al.[21] (Tables 3.2,3.3); and [e] Fitzpatrick & Feldman.[27]

Table 3.16—Percentage Distribution of Full-Time Equivalent Staff, United States, 1990		
	All Mental Health Organizations[a]	Freestanding Multiservice Mental Health Organizations[b]
Patient care staff	73.8	73.5
Professional staff	48.5	52.4
Psychiatrists	3.3	2.7
Other physicians	0.7	0.3
Psychologists	4.0	6.4
Social workers	9.5	17.0
Registered nurses	13.8	4.5
Other mental health professionals	14.9	21.0
Physical health professionals and assistants	2.3	0.5
Other mental health workers	25.3	21.1
Administrative clerical and maintenance staff	26.2	26.5
Total	100.0	100.0

Sources: Data from [a] Bourdon et al.[21(Table 6.8)]; [b] Bourdon et al.[21(Table 6.8g)]

not be the most efficient method for many patients, yet remaining in the community may be so highly valued by the client, the family, and the social worker who helps them that the additional cost seems worthwhile.

These attitudes may put the planner in a difficult situation. On the one hand, the planner may conclude that more people can be assisted with limited resources if the economies of scale of dormitory living arrangements can be achieved. From this perspective, home care might be perceived as a luxury form of long-term care. On the other hand, some people would argue that investment in institutional long-term care is investment in a substandard service delivery modality.

In reality, community care cannot be substituted for institutional care if the client's disabilities are extreme. And the planner must seek to ensure that adequate institutional services are available, since the needs of the institutionalized patient are usually greater than those of the home care patient. At the same time, the number of home health visits required by a person with a given level of disability depends largely on the community's values and its generosity; developing the number of visits required under such circumstances is a matter of group process, not science. Therefore, the planner who is oriented toward objective data should focus first on estimating requirements for institutional care.

Swan and Harrington developed a regression equation predicting the number of nursing home beds per 1000 elderly in a given state.[28] The model explained 70% to 80% of the variance in bed supply. However, because it included personal income as a predictor, it tended to unnecessarily classify wealthy states as having a shortage and poor states as not having a shortage.[29]

Need-based approaches to estimating requirements include bed:population ratios, patient:population ratios, and patient day:population ratios. Application of each of these is complicated by the complexities of supply and demand. Supply issues include the variety of institutions that may be delivering long-term care in a given community. Freestanding nursing facilities are present everywhere, of course, but in addition, there may be hospital swing beds, nursing facilities in hospitals, and foster care homes. A second supply factor is state government regulation. On the one hand, nursing homes in some states may not be allowed to admit some patients because they are not considered sufficiently disabled, depending on screening procedures used by the Medicaid program; this situation effectively reduces supply to zero for some types of cases. On the other hand, shortages of nursing home beds may have been created in some states by refusal of certificates of need. All of these supply issues, plus local demand factors such as climate and culture, per capita income, and the generosity of the Medicaid program, combine to determine utilization of institutional long-term care. As a result, the number of nursing home beds per 1000 elderly varies dramatically among the states.

Given all of these complexities, the planner is forced to fall back on locally derived norms. A local survey will be necessary to enumerate the providers of institutional long-term care and obtain their operating statistics. Then rates per population can be computed. These rates will then be multiplied by the projected population of elderly to obtain future service requirements.

Conclusion

Methods available for use by planners grow steadily more crude as we progress from hospital planning to ambulatory care and long-term care. This is not because planning issues are different but because there is a lack of detailed national, regional, and state information on which to base service requirements and productivity norms. In fact, the dearth of data even extends to enumeration of providers and quantities of services provided. Estimates of requirements for both hospital and nonhospital services will remain crude and labor-intensive until better public information systems are developed.

Despite limitations in the administrative information systems from which planners obtain data, calculations can be made that will give the board a general idea about extreme shortages or surpluses. Even if perfect data were available, no strictly scientific assessment of need or estimation of resource requirements is possible. This is because decisions about service priorities are determined by values as well as data.

REFERENCES

1. *Vital statistics of the United States, 1991, II: part B.* Hyattsville, Md: National Center for Health Statistics; 1995: Table 8-9. DHHS publication PHS 95-1102.
2. *Sam-Graph Pandora.* Lebanon, NH: Codman Research Group Inc; 1994.
3. Institute of Medicine. *Access to Health Care in America.* Washington, DC: National Academy Press; 1993.
4. *Medicine in Transition: Strategies for Change.* Chicago, Ill: American Medical Association; 1995.
5. *Health, United States, 1994.* Hyattsville, Md: National Center for Health Statistics; 1995: Table 83. DHHS publication PHS 95-1232.
6. Dever GE Alan. *Community Health Analysis: Global Awareness at the Local Level.* 2nd ed. Gaithersburg, Md: Aspen; 1991.
7. *American Hospital Association Hospital Statistics 1994–95.* Chicago, Ill: American Hospital Association; 1994: Table 5A.
8. *American Hospital Association Hospital Statistics 1994–95.* Chicago, Ill: American Hospital Association; 1994: Table 5C.

9.   Donabedian A. *Aspects of Medical Care Administration*. Cambridge, Mass: Harvard University Press; 1973.

10.   Griffith JR. Measuring service areas and forecasting demand. In: Griffith JR, Hancock WR, Munson FC, eds. *Cost Control in Hospitals*. Ann Arbor, Mich: Health Administration Press; 1976. p. 36–69.

11.   Shonick W. Elements of planning for area-wide personal health services. St. Louis, Mo: Mosby; 1976.

12.   Rice JA, Creel GH. *Market-Based Demand Forecasting for Inpatient Services*. Chicago, Ill: American Hospital Association; 1985.

13.   Garnick DW, Luft HS, Robinson JC, Tetreault J. Appropriate measures of hospital market areas. *Health Serv Res*. 1987;22:69–89.

14.   Roemer R, Kramer C, Frink JE, Roemer MI. *Planning Urban Health Services: From Jungle to System*. New York, NY: Springer Publishing Co; 1975.

15.   *The National Ambulatory Medical Care Survey, United States 1975–81 and 1985 Trends*. Series 13, No. 93. Hyattsville, Md: National Center for Health Statistics; 1988. DHHS publication PHS 88-1754.

16.   *Current Estimates from the National Health Interview Survey*. Series 10, No. 166. Hyattsville, Md: National Center for Health Statistics; 1987: Table 71. DHHS publication PHS 88-1594.

17.   Kindig DA, Movassaghi H. The adequacy of physician supply in small rural counties. *Health Aff (Millwood)*. Summer 1989:63–75.

18.   Bureau of Health Professions. *Health Personnel in the United States: Ninth Report to Congress*. Rockville, Md: Health Resources and Services Administration; 1993. DHHS publication P-0D-94-1.

19.   *Use of Short-Term General Hospitals by Patients with Psychiatric Diagnoses*. Hospital Cost and Utilization Project Research Note 8. Hyattsville, Md: National Center for Health Services Research; Hospital Studies Program; October 1985. DHHS publication PHS 86-3395.

20.   Rabkin JG. Mental health needs assessment: a review of methods. *Med Care*. 1986;24:1093–1109.

21.   Bourdon KH, Rae DS, Narrow WE, Manderscheid RW, Regier DA. National prevalence and treatment of mental and addictive disorders. In: Manderscheid RW, Sonnenschein MA, eds. *Mental health, United States, 1994*. Washington, DC: US Government Printing Office; 1994. DHHS publication SMA 94-3000.

22.   Wells KB, Keeler E, Manning WG Jr. Patterns of outpatient mental health care over time: some implications for estimates of demand and for benefit design. *Health Serv Res*. 1990;24:773–789.

23.   Sturm R, Jackson CA, Meredith LS, et al. Mental health care utilization in prepaid and fee-for-service plans among depressed patients in the medical outcomes study. *Health Serv Res*. 1995;30:319–340.

24. Knesper DJ, Belcher BE, Cross JG. Variations in the intensity of psychiatric treatment across markets for mental health services in the United States. *Health Serv Res.* 1988;22:797–819.

24. Taube CA, Kessler LG, Burns BJ. Estimating the probability and level of mental health services use. *Health Serv Res (Part II).* 1986;21:321–340.

25. Horgan C. The demand for ambulatory mental health services from specialty providers. *Health Serv Res (Part II).* 1986;21:291–319.

26. Wells KB, Manning WG, Benjamin B. Use of outpatient mental health services in HMO and fee-for-service plans: results from a randomized controlled trial. *Health Serv Res.* 1986;21:453–474.

27. Fitzpatrick RJ, Feldman JL, eds. *Managed Mental Health Care.* Washington, DC: American Psychiatric Press Inc; 1992.

28. Swan JH, Harrington C. Estimating undersupply of nursing home beds in states. *Health Serv Res.* 1986;21:57–83.

29. Rohrer JE. Access to nursing home care: a need-based approach. *Med Care.* 1987;25:796–800.

Chapter 4

Measuring Health System Performance

▨▨▨▨▨▨ HE INFORMATION SYSTEM REQUIRED by the managed primary
▨▨▨ ▨▨▨ care network will encompass the kinds of data used in
▨▨▨▨▨▨ population-based planning (described in chapter 3). It
will also permit the network to monitor its performance, with
performance defined as delivering high-priority services directed
at community health needs. It is important to note that monitoring
utilization rates to ensure that community needs are met also
allows the organization to achieve financial control. In a capitated
system, controlling utilization of services is at least as critical as
controlling the cost per unit of service.

At first glance, it might appear that the same information
used to identify community needs (i.e., morbidity, mortality,
consumer perceptions) can serve to document performance.
However, this is not uniformly the case, because most indicators
of community health status are not sensitive to changes in the
service delivery system. For example, high morbidity levels in a
migrant farm labor population cannot be eliminated by increased
access to primary care. However, increased access can be
measured in terms of visits per capita, documenting that the
network has directed its resources where they are needed.
Exceptions to these rules can be found, of course. Infant mortality
rates and low birthweights, for example, can be influenced by
prenatal care.

Modern health planning, whether governmental or
private sector, generally lacks sufficient regulatory power to
impose rationality. However, planners can and do evaluate
system performance—efficiency, accessibility, and quality.
Indeed, it is an important responsibility of the public health
system to do so. The planner is uniquely qualified to design and
interpret performance monitoring systems that can be used to

redirect resources, help local governments decide what to subsidize and what not to subsidize, and shine the spotlight of the press on areas where quality and efficiency are in doubt.

Unfortunately, health planning is out of fashion. The common perception is that it has been tried in the United States without success. However, the thrust of this book has been toward the conclusion that an epidemiological approach to health systems planning is needed. Therefore, the purpose of this chapter is to offer specific suggestions on how regional and local health system performance can be monitored. The goal for the reader should be to identify indicators for possible inclusion in practical report cards that governing boards will use to ensure accountability. Indeed, achieving accountability can be seen as the hallmark of a well-managed health care system.

Performance Measures

For the purposes of this book, the objectives of the system delivering personal health services are assumed to be accessibility, productivity, quality, and cost containment. One of the first tasks facing the health planner is the selection of performance measures that will enable the planner to answer the question, Is the system achieving its objectives?

Many measures have been used to describe national, regional, and local health system performance. However, the meaning of these measures is rarely discussed. The purpose of this chapter is to catalog the types of indicators available to the planner and their possible uses and to identify a set of measures having practical applications in health planning.

Donabedian has offered a model for evaluating the supply of health services that is useful to planners (see Figure 4.1).[1] Health care resources, such as provider organizations and health care personnel, produce personal health services. The services produced may have some impact on clients' health status, depending on their quality (both effectiveness and appropriateness). Actual need, or health status, influences client perceptions of need for care after being filtered by client attitudes. The attitudes of providers influence their judgments of need for

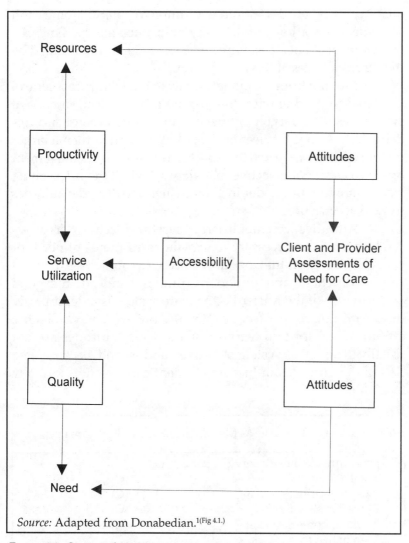

Source: Adapted from Donabedian.[1(Fig 4.1.)]

FIGURE 4.1. System objectives as intervening factors.

care in a similar fashion. The interaction of clients and providers leads to a decision about whether to seek care. The client's ability to use services is determined by the accessibility of those services.

One of the advantages of this model is that it reveals system objectives to be intervening factors between elements of the model. The quantity of resources required to produce needed services depends on their productivity—a system objective. The quantity of resources required to improve population health status depends on both productivity and service quality. Similarly, the ability of clients to acquire needed services is determined by the services' accessibility.

Missing from the model is cost control. While cost control is related to productivity, the two are not identical, since total system costs are largely influenced by the volume of services delivered. And if services are not of high quality, then a larger quantity may be required to correct errors. In short, achievement of the cost control objective may depend on all the intervening factors shown in the model, including client and provider attitudes toward service use.

Attitudes were not listed as system objectives. Yet they can be seen to be necessary to explain assessments of need for care. This suggests that the list of objectives should be expanded to include client and provider attitudes. Indeed, the good performance of the Kaiser Permanente system is at least partly due to attitude control (see chapter 5). However, we will ignore attitudes here for two reasons: first, because attitudes are not usually included as system objectives, and second, because data describing attitudes influencing patient care are not normally available.

Table 4.1—Health Costs as Measures of System Performance

Expenditures on health services per capita	
Total	(C)
Hospital services	(C)
Physician services	(C)
Nursing home services	(C)
Mental health services	(C)
Other services	(C)
Expenditures as % of GDP or GNP	(C)
Changes in health expenditures (inflation)	(C)
Provider-based measures	(C)
Hospital cost per case	(C,P)
Cost per patient day	(C,P)

Note: Letters in parentheses indicate which aspects of performance are measured. A = access; C = cost control; P = productivity; Q = quality.

We might expect that Figure 4.1 could be used to classify measures of system performance. Ideally, the various indicators available to the planner could be classified by system objectives. Specifically, some indicators might measure the performance of the system in regard to cost containment, others in regard to productivity, and the remainder in regard to accessibility or quality. Perusal of Tables 4.1 through 4.5, however, quickly reveals that performance measures cannot easily be classified according to objectives. Instead, many indicators have been employed to measure more than one aspect of performance. Therefore, performance indicators will be classified here according to the kinds of data used to compute them. A subset of provider-based measures is included at the end of each of the first four tables. The conceptual problems of these measures will be discussed at length later in this chapter.

Table 4.1 lists examples of several types of cost data that have been used as measures of system performance. Most could be said to measure total system cost and therefore could be used to indicate the degree to which the cost control objective has been met. Most of them are valid for that purpose if properly adjusted for demographic factors. However, gross cost, unadjusted for population changes, measures very little.

Some cost measures have been interpreted as relating to objectives other than productivity or cost containment. For example, when costs are computed on a per capita basis they might be used to indicate the accessibility of care in different areas or for different populations. The assumption here would be that equal expenditures indicate equal value received. Therefore, per capita costs may have to be adjusted for differences in wage rates or cost of living. Per capita expenditures may also be used to indicate whether unhealthy populations are actually receiving more services than healthy populations. For example, are medical expenditures per poor person per year greater than those for the average person in the middle class? The question being addressed in this case clearly relates to whether equitable access to care has been achieved. In general, however, per capita expenditures reflect cost containment and productivity, not accessibility.

Two cost measures might be interpreted as indicators of productivity. Cost per patient day and cost per case both represent inputs per unit of output—the definition of productivity. At the same time, lower costs per case and per patient day would be taken to indicate that costs are being controlled if one can assume that volume is under control. Clearly, productivity and total cost are related.

Finally, the reader should note that some analysts would interpret low expenditures as evidence of a poor quality health system, under the assumption that better care will cost more. For example, if a developing nation spends only 10% as much per capita on personal health services as the United States, perhaps this indicates that the quality of personal health services its residents receive is inferior to that received by Americans. Of course, the analyst would hasten to add that this is a crude measure of quality, since most planners assume that a great deal of waste and inefficiency exists in the US system. Therefore, 10 times as large an expenditure may not indicate 10 times as much quality. Nevertheless, if the differences are great enough, higher cost may sometimes indicate higher quality. For the most part,

Table 4.2—Health Resources as Measures of System Performance	
Hospital beds per 1000 population	(A)
Primary care physicians per 1000 population	(A)
Specialists per 1000 population	(A)
Nurses per 1000 population	(A)
Mental health professionals per 1000 population	(A)
Dentists per 1000 population	(A)
Pharmacists per 1000 population	(A)
Total health personnel per 1000 population	(A)
Nursing home beds per 1000 population	(A)
Provider-based measures	
Ratio of full-time employees to average daily census	(C,P,Q)
Ratio of clinical staff to patient visits per week	(P)
Ratio of clinical staff to enrolled patients	(C)

Note: Letters in parentheses indicate which aspects of performance are measured. A = access; C = cost control; P = productivity; Q = quality.

however, there is rarely a good justification for using cost data to draw conclusions about either access or quality.

Table 4.2 shows various measures of health resources that have been used as indicators of system performance. The interpretation of these indicators, even when properly adjusted for demographic factors, is quite problematic. If one system has fewer hospital beds per 1000 than another system, for example, the lower number could be taken as evidence of greater productivity, if the two systems serve the same size populations. This assumes, of course, that areas with fewer beds are meeting local needs as well as areas with more beds. Fewer beds per 1000 also indicates better cost control, both because of lower capital investment and because excess capacity is thought to generate unnecessary hospital use. If the number of beds per capita are too low, however, access may be reduced.

A similar chain of reasoning can be applied to human resources. In addition, a shortage of any particular type of essential personnel might be interpreted as indicating substandard quality, because it suggests that some kinds of care are being delivered by unqualified staff or are not being delivered at all.

The most reasonable interpretation of resource rates is as indicators of access. However, access is a very complex concept. Accessibility can refer to the quantitative adequacy of resources (e.g., beds per capita), the affordability of care, the amenability of the system to service use by people who need care, the acceptability of care once it is received, and distance to care.[1] Clearly, most of these types of access are not likely to be measurable with available data.

The ratio of clinical staff to patient visits can be thought of as relating inputs (staff) to outputs (visits). Therefore, it is a measure of productivity. A high ratio of clinical staff to enrollees suggests overinvestment and thus failure to control costs.

Utilization measures (Table 4.3) have also been used for a variety of purposes. These measures should usually be adjusted for age, sex, and race. Higher utilization means that more services have been produced and so might be taken as a measure of productivity. However, there is no measure of input in a utilization rate and therefore, since productivity is defined as the quantity of output relative to input, utilization rates are not true measures of productivity.

Table 4.3—Health Services Utilization Rates as Measures of System Performance

Procedure rates, selected procedures	(A,C)
Office visits per 1000 population	(A,C)
Hospital admissions per 1000 population	(A,C,Q)
Hospital patient days per 1000 population	(A,C)
Emergency room visits per 1000 population	(A,C,Q)
Prenatal visits per birth	(A,C,Q)
Abortion rates	(A,C)
Nursing home days per 1000 population	(A,C)
Nursing home residents per 1000 population	(A,C)
Home health visits per 1000 population	(A,C)
Mental health visits per 1000 population	(A,C)
Substance abuse visits per 1000 population	(A,C)
Provider-based measures	
Occupancy rate	(C,P)
Average length of stay	(C,P)
Retention rate	(Q)
Market share	(Q)
Office visits per year per physician	(P)
Average duration of office visits	(A,C,P,Q)
Commitment index	(Q)

Note: Letters in parentheses indicate which aspects of performance are measured. A = access; C = cost control; P = productivity; Q = quality.

Utilization rates are sometimes used as evidence of cost control, with higher rates indicating that costs are not being controlled. This interpretation assumes that differences in wage rates and other production costs that may vary geographically are not as important for planning purposes as differences in quantities of service.

Utilization rates are perhaps most often used as measures of accessibility. The assumption here is that if services are being used they must be accessible. On the other hand, low utilization rates may not be taken as proof of access barriers; after all, they may represent client preferences. In general, however, utilization rates are probably the best measures of access that can be acquired without special population surveys.

Utilization of some kinds of services can be used as a measure of quality.[2] Too few prenatal visits indicates poor quality. Heavy use of neonatal intensive care units is evidence of poor quality if this use results from inadequate prenatal care. High rates of emergency room use or hospitalization for some conditions, such as uncontrolled diabetes, can be attributed to lack of primary care. However, the planner must recognize that some episodes of care that could have been prevented result from patient intransigence that no amount of public health education could overcome. Therefore, utilization rates are valid measures of system quality only in rare cases.

Data describing hospital activity levels are more readily available than most potential performance measures because they are published annually by the American Hospital Association. These indicators have been interpreted in a variety of ways. Occupancy rate has been used as a rough proxy for financial viability, for example. A high occupancy rate can mean that a hospital is productive or that it is controlling its costs. However, direct measurement of hospital financial viability would be far more accurate, because often not all reported beds are actually staffed, thus causing the occupancy rate to appear lower than it actually is.

Market share has been touted as the best measure of a hospital's ability to serve its community well.[3] The assumption here is that community residents will notice poor service and use other hospitals as a result. Of course, it is entirely possible that clients will not always know good care from bad or that there will be a considerable lag between the time care begins to deteriorate and the loss of market share.

A high volume of hospital activity has been interpreted as indicating both productivity and evidence of quality. At the same time, high volume may mean that the hospital is accessible and achieving lower costs due to economies of scale. On the other hand, high volume could mean that the community is being overserved. Clearly, cost control within the hospital is not the same as cost control from a system perspective.

All things considered, volume data should not be taken as evidence of productivity, access, cost control, or quality because they are not expressed as ratios relative to need for care. Exceptions would be volumes of specific procedures in which outcomes are known to be sensitive to volume.

Some population-oriented measures can be computed from provider data. For example:

- The retention rate is the proportion of the population not traveling outside of the area for care.
- The commitment index is the proportion of the hospital's patient load that comes from the local area. A high commitment index may indicate that the hospital is not serving a broad area. This measure may be described as a dependency rate, because it indicates that the hospital is dependent on the local area for patients.
- Discharges per capita is computed from patient origin and destination data by attributing hospital use to a population regardless of where care was received. This is a utilization measure that depends on provider data.

Table 4.4—Health Status Indicators as Measures of System Performance

Years of productive life lost due to illness	(A,Q)
Lost wages and medical care costs due to illness	(A,C)
Mortality rates	
Infant	(A)
Neonatal	(A)
Perinatal	(A)
Maternal	(A,Q)
Heart attacks	(A,Q)
Trauma	(A,Q)
Life expectancy	*
Quality-adjusted life years/well years	*
Morbidity rates	
Acute conditions	*
Chronic conditions	*
Disability days and activity restriction	*
Preventable diseases	(A,Q)
Provider-based measures	
Case fatality	(Q)
Hospital readmissions	(Q)

Note: Letters in parentheses indicate which aspects of performance are measured. A = access; C = cost control; P = productivity; Q = quality.

* These health status indicators are generally not valid measures of health system performance unless particular programs are targeted at them for narrowly-defined populations.

- Beds per capita is computed by attributing hospital beds to a population in a manner proportionate to its use of each hospital. This is a resource measure that depends on provider data.

These indicators are unusual, however. Most provider-based measures describe the activities of the service providers independently of the populations they serve. The validity of these measures in comparison with population-based measures is discussed at the end of this chapter.

The meaning of health status indices as measures of system performance (Table 4.4) is especially difficult to divine. Poor population health status can be taken as evidence that more health services are needed. At the same time, planners may try to interpret poor population health status as evidence that the health system is unproductive or of poor quality, suggesting that a better job could be done within existing resources.[4-7] In short, planners may be left in a quandary about whether to expand or constrain resources in the face of poor population health status.

While some analysts have defined poor population health status as a system outcome indicating poor performance, all recognize that many factors besides the health system may be at fault. For example, poor nutrition, inadequate housing, and limited education may have more to do with population health status than the quantity or quality of personal health services.

On the other hand, some adverse events are known to be preventable by well-organized and adequately funded health systems. Infant mortality is a good example, as are deaths due to traumatic injuries or heart attacks. Therefore, health status should not be used as an indicator of system quality unless the

---

Table 4.5—Provider Characteristics as Measures of System Performance

Hospital accreditation	(Q)
Hospitals with specified facilities and services	(C)
Location (distance)	(A)
Financial viability	(C)

Note: Letters in parentheses indicate which aspects of performance are measured. A = access; C = cost control; P = productivity; Q = quality.

measure relates patient outcomes to narrowly defined preventive services or treatments. Health status does not measure access either, unless it is used to quantify a population in need of a particular kind of care. Even then, it is meaningful only when it is paired with resources (e.g., doctors) or service use in the form of a ratio.

A few kinds of useful provider data are available at the regional level in the United States (Table 4.5). Hospital accreditation is known. However, accreditation merely verifies the existence of minimum levels of quality.

The number of facilities and services provided by hospitals in a region is also published. These data allow planners to judge how broadly dispersed services are, which is a reflection of cost control as well as access. For example, if cardiac catheterization is available at several hospitals in a region, it may be taken as an indication of excessive access, raising production costs and probably leading to unnecessarily high utilization rates. The reported availability of facilities and services can be misleading, however, because the volume of services delivered by a given hospital is usually not known; just because a hospital reports providing home care does not mean that it provides home care in sufficient volume to meet community needs. Therefore, knowledge of the distribution of facilities and services tells more about cost containment than about access.

Knowledge of provider location permits computation of distance to care, which measures access. Excessive access may indicate failure to control costs. Like facilities and services, distance can be misleading because it does not reflect quantities of resources. Short distances to care may create the appearance of ready access, but if clinics and hospitals are understaffed or otherwise have insufficient capacity, then access is not as great as it might appear.

Financial viability might be taken as direct evidence that hospitals and clinics have produced in sufficient volume to achieve scale economies and have minimized cost per case. However, this is not the same as saying the cost to society has been minimized, since providers may charge high prices even if their costs are low. Furthermore, costs may be high for reasons beyond the provider's control. Therefore, an essential clinic or hospital may be expensive, but it may be that there is no less expensive way to provide services to the population in question.

Population-Based vs Provider-Based Measures

The problem of judging the need for a provider organization, such as a hospital, can be approached either from the perspective of the provider or from the perspective of the population. From the provider's perspective, the need for the hospital's services is reflected by the demands directed toward it. If planners assume that local physicians order services only when needed and that all needs are brought to the attention of the physicians, then utilization is a reasonable proxy for need. Furthermore, utilization may also reveal patients' priorities. From this perspective, patient preferences are more important than judgments of community need made by state planners.

The crux of the provider approach to assessing need for the hospital lies in demonstrated levels of activity. For example, if the acute inpatient services of a hospital are frequently used, then continuation of the inpatient role is appropriate. Conversely, if the volume of acute inpatient services is negligible, then the community has no great need for that hospital to provide those services.

The provider perspective assumes that need and demand are congruent and that physicians and patients are reliable judges of need. A public health perspective finds these assumptions untenable. Clients are not rational about their use of health services for several reasons: (1) insurance lets them avoid the cost of care; (2) need for care is accompanied by anxiety and pain; (3) use of service is often unpleasant; (4) need for care is sometimes unexpected and may occur when clients are least able to afford it; (5) the consequences of poor choices, such as the decision to engage in unhealthy behavior, are often deferred; (6) clients have limited information on which to base their decisions; and (7) after the initial contact with the health system has been made, many if not most decisions are made by providers rather than clients.[1]

The limitations of patient assessments of their own medical needs should be apparent; after all, patients seek professional help in making decisions about their use of health services. And the entire field of public health education is directed at public ignorance about when care should be sought and how to prevent the need for care.

The assumption that use of services reflects need because physicians control utilization is controversial. Many studies have demonstrated "unexplainable" geographic variations in medical treatment. This body of literature has led to widespread acceptance of what might be described as the practice style hypothesis: geographic variations in service use are due to erratic physician behavior rather than variations in medical need.[8] While it is true that measurement of practice style has proven difficult, the practice style hypothesis has become generally accepted.

Geographic variations in treatment would never have been discovered had planners adhered to the provider perspective; in fact, such variations are exacerbated when planners use provider-based data.[8] Needed instead is a population perspective, in which the treatment experience of the population is measured regardless of the location of the provider. In the 1970s, when the federal government was engaged in health planning, experts were urging the substitution of population-based standards for utilization-based standards. However, even as late as 1982, Shaughnessy was able to observe that even though per capita performance measures are conceptually superior, they are rarely used for decision-making.[9] Inadequate data, political barriers, and technical issues have all contributed to this deficiency.

Analysts have sought to resolve the conflict between the provider and population perspectives by defining service areas for hospitals. If a service area can be defined that matches a population with a hospital, and if demographic and health status data can be obtained for that area, then utilization rates can be computed that are true reflections of both the demand experienced by the hospital and the behavior of the population.

The Wennberg studies of geographic variations in service use have assigned very small areas, such as zip codes, to particular hospitals to form service areas.[8] However, regardless of the method used to make the assignments, a certain percentage of residents will migrate out of the service area for treatment. The net effect is that the treatment experience of the population is not perfectly congruent with the utilization of the local hospital.

Griffith attempted to resolve this problem by constructing service populations rather than service areas.[10] In this method, a fraction of each small area's population, rather than the entire population, was assigned to the hospital's service population. While this method is conceptually appealing, it assumes that the assignment of a fraction of the small area's population to the hospital accurately reflects where people would go for care if they became ill.[11]

Garnick et al. reviewed the methods used to construct service areas and concluded that none were ideal but that some were more appropriate for some purposes than others.[12] For example, because it constitutes a relevant geopolitical unit, the county as service area may be appropriate for a policy study, provided that efforts are made to correct for migration out of the county for treatment.

Not least among the methodological difficulties associated with the population-based perspective is the measurement of the population's need for health care.[13] Synthetic estimates of the health status of county populations can be developed. However, such estimates should not be used to estimate quantities of health services needed, because they are simply functions of the demographic characteristics of the population. Demographic factors alone are too crude to permit accurate assessment of need for care. Surveys can be done to collect morbidity data describing the prevalence of chronic illness, but these rates cannot readily be converted into quantities of health services needed. Mortality rates and the incidence of reportable diseases suffer from the same deficiency.

In short, an argument can be made for the conceptual superiority of population-based indicators. However, limitations of data and methods impede exclusive reliance on such measures. Furthermore, the requirement for preserving local control over the planning process lends value to the provider-based indicators.

Table 4.6—Health Plan Employer Data and Information Set (HEDIS): Major Quality Indicators

Childhood immunizations
Cholesterol screening
Mammograms
Pap smears
Prenatal care
Retinal screen for diabetics
Follow-up after hospitalization for major affective disorder
Percentage of members who visit provider
Asthma admission rate
Low birthweight rate
Physician turnover
Utilization rates
    Coronary bypass
    Angioplasty
    Cardiac catheterization
    Cholecystectomy
    Hysterectomy
    Prostatectomy
    Laminectomy
    Cesarean sections
    Readmission for chemical dependency
    Obstetric hospital stay
    Hospital days per 1000 population

Source: National Committee for Quality Assurance.[14]

Recommended Performance Indicators

The overall performance of the primary care system can be monitored by means of a standard approach derived from the health services research literature, though specific indicators can be expected to evolve over time. A commonly used approach (see Table 4.6) is reflected in the Health Plan Employer Data and Information Set (HEDIS).[14] The HEDIS is similar to a set of indicators recommended by the Institute of Medicine (IOM) that reflect progress toward national objectives (see Table 4.7).[15] The objectives are as follows: (1) promoting successful birth outcomes, (2) reducing the incidence of vaccine-preventable childhood

Table 4-7—Indicators Proposed by the Institute of Medicine
Adequacy of prenatal care[a] (A,Q) Infant mortality rate (A,Q) Percentage low birthweight (A,Q) Congenital syphilis rate (A,Q) Preschool immunization percentage (A,Q) Incidence of vaccine-preventable childhood diseases (A,Q) Breast and cervical cancer screening rates (A,Q) Incidence of late-stage breast and cervical cancer (A,Q) Continuing care for chronic diseases (average number of physician contacts per year for those in fair or poor health[a]; proportion with no physician contacts) (A) High-cost discretionary care (admission rates for referral-sensitive procedures) (A,C,Q) Avoidable hospitalization for chronic diseases (admissions for ambulatory care–sensitive chronic conditions) (A,C,Q) Access-related excess mortality[a] (A,Q) Acute medical care (percentage of individuals with no physician contact) (A) Dental services (average number of dental visits per year) (A) Avoidable hospitalizations for Acute Conditions (admission rates for ambulatory care–sensitive conditions) (A,C,Q)
Note: Letters in parenthesis indicate which aspects of care are measured. A = access; C = cost; Q = quality. [a] Not readily measured from secondary data *Source*: The Institute of Medicine.[15]

diseases, (3) increasing the early detection and diagnosis of treatable diseases, (4) reducing the effects of chronic disease and prolonging life, and (5) reducing morbidity and pain through timely and appropriate treatment. The IOM data set draws heavily on claims data to compute rates.

Medical care utilization rates have been used as quality indicators for several decades. For example, Paul Lembcke pioneered the use of regional utilization rates as indicators of hospital quality by showing that teaching hospitals were less likely than outlying community hospitals to perform appendectomies.[16] Furthermore, teaching hospitals' service areas also experienced lower appendicitis death rates. The utilization rate approach to measuring quality was popularized by Wennberg

Table 4.8—Supplemental Performance Indicators

Hospital beds per capita (A,C)
Travel time to hospitals (A)
Primary care personnel per capita (A)
Specialty physicians per capita (A,C)
Nurses per capita (A)
Pharmacists per capita (A)
Travel time to primary care (A)
Dentists per capita (A)
Nursing home beds per 1000 people aged 85 years and over (A,C)
Inpatient residential treatment beds in mental health organizations per 100,000 population (A,C)
Home health visits per 1000 elderly (A,C)
Licensed mental health providers per capita (A)
EMS response time (A)
Hospital utilization rates for high-cost procedures (A,C)
Hospital expenditures per capita (C)
Physician expenditures per capita (C)
Primary care expenditures per capita (C)
Specialty physician expenditures per capita (C)
Total health care expenditures per capita (C)
Dental expenditures per capita (C)
Mental health expenditures per capita (C)
Dental expenditures per capita (C)
EMS expenditures per capita (C)
Volume in volume–sensitive conditions (Q)
Client satisfaction (A,Q)
Substance abuse expenditures per capita (C)

Note: Letters in parentheses indicate which aspects of care are measured. A = access; C = cost; Q = quality; EMS = emergency medical service.

and others in the United States and by Roos and others in Canada.[8,17,18]

The IOM indicators do not address the availability and accessibility of all types of medical care. Examples of other useful indicators include travel time to hospitals and primary care, primary care providers per capita, and emergency medical service response time (see Table 4.8). Number of nursing home beds per 1000 residents 85 years of age and older and number of inpatient and residential treatment beds in mental health organizations per 100 000 population were suggested by Aday et al. as supplemental indicators of "potential access."[19]

Also missing from the IOM indicators are surveys of client satisfaction with the quality and accessibility of services. The IOM report recommended that additional indicators be developed in the following areas: HIV/AIDS care, substance abuse services; care for migrants, homeless people, and people with disabilities; family violence; emergency services; post–acute care services for the elderly; and prescription drugs.[15]

Indicators of the types listed in Tables 4.7 and 4.8 are only that—indicators. They cannot offer positive proof of poor performance of primary care systems. Instead, they serve as a screening mechanism. When indicator values are different from standards, closer investigation should be undertaken to verify the findings.

Careful consideration of the indicators shown in Tables 4.7 and 4.8 reveals that they are surprisingly easy to assemble. Investment in expensive software packages is not required. If the local hospital can generate discharges by diagnosis, these can be matched with population and referral-sensitive conditions. Other indicators are even more easily computed.

Not mentioned to this point are indicators of financial performance, such as cost per case, net revenue, and hospital length of stay. While these measures are relevant to financial management of an institution such as a hospital, they are less relevant to performance of a primary care system in which the hospital is a contributory member. The drivers of system costs are utilization rates; controlling cost per unit is a problem for the hospitals, group practices, and other member agencies. Most system costs are generated by utilization of specialty services outside the primary care system. If specialty utilization can be controlled, then cost control by local providers will be less urgent. In short, performance indicators relevant to financial control might include the following: total physician visits per 1000, specialty visits per 1000, hospitalizations per 1000, emergency department visits per 1000, total expenditures per 1000, and cost of health insurance premiums.

This minimalist approach to management information systems is at odds with most expert opinion. The growth of managed care has given rise to calls for replacing claims data (not needed for payment in capitated systems) with encounter data. Encounter information can be even more detailed than claims data, possibly erasing the "administrative costs dividend" proponents of managed care hoped to achieve by eliminating fee-for-service care. Such detailed information may be useful at regional headquarters, but it is less so at the local level where the number of cases of any given type is small. I remain unconvinced that detailed clinical information will save more than it costs to collect.

Mental Health and Substance Abuse Services

The literature cited above suggests a set of indicators that may be useful for monitoring the performance of mental health and substance abuse treatment systems. It is worth repeating

---

Table 4.9—Proposed Performance Indicators for Evaluation of Managed Mental Health and Substance Abuse Treatment

Structural indicators
    Psychiatrist FTEs per 1000 clients
    Counselor FTEs per 1000 clients
    Case manager FTEs per 1000 clients
    Other support staff FTEs per 1000 clients

Process indicators (utilization rates)
    Number of counseling sessions per 1000 clients
    Number of individual counseling sessions per 1000 clients
    Number of group counseling sessions per 1000 clients
    Number of family counseling sessions per 1000 clients

Outcome indicators
    Number of hospitalizations per 1000 clients
    Percentage hospitalized
    Number emergency room visits per 1000 clients
    Percentage completing recommended course of treatment
    Percentage having a prior admission

Note: Each set of indicators can be calculated separately for high-risk clients, for lower-risk clients, and for all clients. FTE = full-time equivalent.

that we are assuming that the providers are responsible for system performance in all of its dimensions, not just cost control. Incentives directed at ensuring access and quality will be needed.

Proposed indicators are shown in Table 4.9. Seriously dependent (high-risk) individuals can be identified by means of an algorithm based on readmission, history of drug use, criminal history, and psychiatric comorbidities, thus allowing separate analysis of other clients. This constitutes a crude case-mix adjustment. Nevertheless, many unmeasured client differences could affect outcomes. Therefore, the proposed indicators are intended for use only as screens. They are *indicators* of performance, not proof positive. At the same time, they are sufficiently valid to justify asking a managed care contractor to explain why performance appears to be suboptimal.

The separation of enrollees with chronic problems or high-risk clients from the general enrollee population poses an interesting methodological problem. If, for example, all counselors are counted in the numerator of both the chronic or high-risk case rate and the general rate, then double-counting has occurred. On the other hand, how would some counselors be allocated to the chronic or high-risk clients and others to the general population? A simple solution is to use the proportion of contact hours for each type of case. This allocation method can be applied to the structural, process, and outcome indicators shown in Table 4.9.

Staff hours (structural indicators) can be allocated to different types of enrollees on the basis of the number of claims filed. Staff hours per enrollee can be classified by type of personnel. The availability of counselors is an important dimension of the accessibility of services. The amount of resources devoted to case management, as reflected by case manager full-time equivalents, is also important. A minimalist approach to this function could consist entirely of the centralized utilization review. However, client outcomes are likely to be better if the agency takes a more proactive stance, encouraging outreach and follow-up by treatment agencies to ensure optimal resolution of client problems. It is assumed that the availability of case managers will increase over time. Availability of other types of staff should also be monitored; including unlicensed staff such as those who provide life skills counseling, arrange for transportation, or otherwise aid clients.

Utilization rates serve as process indicators because they reflect how much care people are able to acquire. For example, a small number of counseling sessions may reflect access barriers. At the same time, high rates may suggest inefficiencies in the system or failure to prevent a need for care.

Complete risk adjustment of these rates will often not be feasible. Baseline data collection systems are not standard across states, so risk-adjustment models using other states as comparison groups cannot be developed.

Adherence to the recommended course of treatment (completion of treatment) is a reasonable outcome indicator of system performance. However, providers might be encouraged to set goals that are easily achievable so that they can score well on this indicator. Therefore, it is also necessary to interpret completion rates in light of other outcome indicators.

Two performance indicators (hospitalizations and emergency room visits) relate primarily to adverse consequences of access barriers or ineffective treatment. As with all of the proposed indicators, a single adverse event such as a hospitalization is not interpreted as a failure. However, if the overall rate does not meet standards, then there is some cause for concern. Standards can come from comparable organizations, from organizations regarded as good performers, or from the system's own past performance.

Relapse is a widely used indicator of successful treatment. While no standards have been developed for determining a reasonable recidivism rate, monitoring the percentage of clients admitted for treatment who have previously undergone treatment will determine whether repeat admission rates are changing.

Assessing Public Health Performance

Community-oriented health systems must be integrated with and guided by a public health perspective in order to be effective. In application, this means that specific public health practices must be performed by someone. These practices include conducting needs assessments, identifying behavioral risk factors, performing epidemiological investigations, reviewing public health policies, developing proposed policy changes, ensuring public input, ensuring that local health codes are up to date, monitoring environmental safety, and conducting public health education.

A questionnaire has been developed to assess how well a community is performing these functions.[20] It was field-tested in six states in 1993 and then applied in Iowa in 1995 by surveying local health agency directors. In both surveys, performance averages only about 50%. Performance was worst in planning functions (assess, investigate, prioritize, plan, and evaluate).

Clearly, the capacity of public health systems to provide oversight and direction is limited. The kinds of system performance indicators discussed above must be analyzed by managers who have the community's health as their foremost concern, yet their ability to provide an oversight role is often limited by a lack of resources or expertise. Much work remains to be done. If local management of primary care systems can be achieved with accountability to a community-based governing board, then it is possible that commitment to public health goals will result.

Conclusion

Many of the indicators used as measures of health system performance are valid only if certain assumptions are made. For example, low cost per case indicates control of total costs only if volume is controlled, and, conversely, low utilization per capita indicates cost control only if cost per unit is controlled.

Planners are advised to interpret performance measures with caution. Referring to Figure 4.1 can aid in identification of untenable assumptions. Ultimately, however, the following rules of thumb will prove useful:

1. Never assume that performance measures are perfectly valid.
2. Never assume that the data used to compute performance measures were completely accurate.
3. Never assume that population-based indicators accurately measure the performance of individual providers, or that provider-

based indicators accurately measure the performance of the system. Use population-based measures to describe system performance and provider-based measures to describe the performance of individual providers.

4.   Supplement hard data with informed local judgments when planning for small areas.

5.   Measure total system cost with expenditure data, not charges.

6.   Measure productivity as a ratio of services used to resources available.

7.   Measure accessibility as a ratio of services used to population at risk. These rates should be adjusted for factors known to be related to the need for care.

8.   Use population health status to measure system quality only when firm evidence exists showing that the indicator is reliable and valid. Some sentinel health events can meet this requirement, but global measures, such as life expectancy, may not.

REFERENCES

1.   Donabedian A. *Aspects of Medical Care Administration*. Cambridge, Mass: Harvard University Press; 1973.
2.   Rutstein DD, Berenberg W, Chalmers TC, Child CG, Fishman AP, Perrin EB. Measuring the quality of medical care: a clinical method. *N Engl J Med*. 1976;294:582–588.
3.   Griffith JR. *The Well-Managed Community Hospital*. Ann Arbor, Mich: Health Administration Press; 1987.
4.   Charlton J, Lakhani A, Aristidou M. How have "avoidable death" indices for England and Wales changed: 1974–78 compared with 1979–83. *Community Med*. 1986;8:304–314.
5.   Carr-Hill RA, Hardman GF, Russell IT. Variations in avoidable mortality and variations in health care resources. *Lancet*. 1987;II:789–792.
6.   Charlton J, Velez R. Some international comparison of mortality amenable to medical intervention. *BMJ*. 1986;292:295–301.
7.   Charlton J, Bauer R, Lakhani A. Outcome measures for district and regional health care planners. *Community Med*. 1984;6:306–315.
8.   Wennberg J, Gittelsohn A. Small area variations in health care delivery. *Science*. 1973;182:1102–1107.
9.   Shaughnessy PH. Methodological issues in per capita measurement in health care. *Health Serv Res*. 1982;17:61–80.
10.   Griffith JR. Quantitative techniques for hospital planning and control. Lexington, Mass: D.C. Heath & Co; 1972.
11.   Rohrer JE. Defining service populations for hospitals. *J Health Hum Resour Adm*. 1987;10(2):156–173.

12. Garnick DW, Luft HS, Robinson JC, Tetreault J. Appropriate measures of hospital market areas. *Health Serv Res.* 1987;22(1):69–89.
13. Mooney A, Rives NW. Measures of community health status for health planning. *Health Serv Res.* Summer 1978:129–145.
14. *Report Card Pilot Project.* Washington, DC: National Committee for Quality Assurance; 1995.
15. Institute of Medicine. *Access to Health Care in America.* Washington, DC: National Academy Press; 1993.
16. Lembcke P. Measuring the quality of medical care through vital statistics based on hospital service areas, 1: comparative study of appendectomy rates. *Am J Public Health.* 1952;42:276–286.
17. Roos NP, Lyttle D. The centralization of operations and access to treatment: total hip replacement in Manitoba. *Am J Public Health.* 1985;75:130–133.
18. Roos NP, Sharp SM. Innovation, centralization, and growth: coronary artery bypass graft surgery in Manitoba. *Med Care.* 1989;27:441–452.
19. Aday LA, Begley CE, Lairson DR, Slater CH. Evaluating the medical care system: effectiveness, efficiency, and equity. Ann Arbor, Mich: Health Administration Press; 1993.
20. Richards TB, Rogers JJ, Christenson GM, Miller CA, Taylor MS, Cooper AD. Evaluating local public health performance at a public level on a statewide basis. *J Public Health Manage Pract.* 1995;1(4):70–83.
21. Rohrer JE, Dominguez DG. Public health performance in Iowa's counties. Final report to Iowa Department of Public Health; December 1995; University of Iowa, Iowa City, Iowa. Contract No. 5886CH20.

Chapter 5

Monitoring Quality and Appropriateness

EALTH PLANNERS SHOULD HAVE AT LEAST A BASIC understanding of how managers control quality of care, for four reasons. First, planners will need to interpret reports on the quality of patient care. After all, evaluation of performance precedes plan development. Second, planners may be required to do special studies of quality when the governance system or top management is not satisfied with internally developed data. Third, planners, to the extent that they relate to particular patient care provider organizations, will want to ensure that their plans include recommendations for quality control mechanisms.

Finally, quality assessment includes review of the appropriateness of services delivered. Inappropriate over-treatment wastes scarce resources that could be used for other purposes. Planners who seek to determine what level of investment is needed in a community must be confident that existing services are being used appropriately. However, they are well advised to approach the subjects of quality and appropriateness with delicacy. Clinicians have always been defensive when nonclinicians raise these subjects because clinicians, quite correctly, feel that a high level of clinical knowledge is necessary for the sensible interpretation of data. Administrators of provider organizations may be equally difficult to deal with on the subject of quality. Managerial philosophies about quality improvement seem at times to have acquired the status of ideologies whose proponents are zealots. Yet each decade the current philosophy fades as a new one, marketed by persuasive consultants, captures management's attention.

Before I address the theory and mechanics of monitoring, a clarification of terminology will be helpful. Patient care is of high quality when the process employed can be expected to maximize a broad definition of client welfare.[1] Good care is not wasteful, because more clients can receive care if services are delivered efficiently. Therefore, quality encompasses the notion of appropriateness; only those resources that contribute cost-effectively to patient welfare should be used. Conversely, it would be inappropriate to withhold resources needed for patient care.

Quality assessment is usually distinguished from utilization review because quality assessment has traditionally focused on auditing the process of care employed in individual client-provider interactions, whereas utilization review has focused on analysis of aggregate data to verify that care is appropriate.[2] However, quality assessment can and often should start with aggregate data. In a broad sense, utilization review should be thought of as a type of quality assessment, just as appropriate care is high-quality care. Epidemiological monitoring, or surveillance, is the systematic analysis of quality assessment or utilization review data. Quality Improvement, Total Quality Management, and Continuous Quality Improvement are all newer terms describing approaches that attempt to blend aggregate data, patient-level data, and group processes to improve patient care.

Approaches to Quality Assessment

Classical Quality Assessment

Quality assessment methods have generally been classified into three types: structure, process, and outcome. This formulation was originally offered by Donabedian, who had reviewed the literature extensively.[3] Donabedian's trichotomy has become the textbook standard in quality assessment, along with his observation that valid quality assessment requires the establishment of a link between the process of care and its outcomes.[1] In other words, process measures are not valid if they cannot be shown to affect outcomes and outcome measures are not valid if they are not controllable through good process. In many cases, structure may be the most important determinant of quality; however, structure can generally be disregarded in studies that seek to be precise and timely because structural measures are low in sensitivity (in the statistical sense). In short, quality assessment systems must somehow combine process and outcome measures.

The truth of this observation has shaped the development of quality assessment systems to the point where it may no longer be appropriate to divide quality assessment approaches into process and outcome. Instead, approaches vary in the ways they combine the two. Furthermore, designers of new approaches to quality assessment will have the opportunity to make use of detailed clinical databases that were not previously available. This chapter attempts to identify some new directions in quality assessment that may be employed either at the system level or within health care delivery organizations.

The Traditional Quality Assessment Approach

All approaches to quality assessment require the identification of problems or suspected problems, study of those problems, corrective action, and reevaluation to verify problem resolution. The traditional approach to quality assessment in health care involves the identification of problems through clinical judgment (although other data sources may be employed if they are confirmed by clinical judgment), the development of process criteria by way of consensus among relevant clinical specialties, and the use of these criteria to review medical records. Often the suspected problem is determined to be explainable by the circumstances of the cases reviewed, to the great relief of all concerned. When action is taken, it usually takes the form of seminars or other types of clinical reeducation. The weaknesses of this approach are (1) weak problem identification, leading to studies (called medical audits) that are not directed at true problems; (2) a tendency to fail to identify some problems because so much effort is consumed in audits of narrowly defined problems; (3) a tendency to focus on problems that are bothersome to staff rather than to patients; and (4) an understandable tendency to err on the side of vindicating current process. As a result, the quality assessment system is inefficient in terms of corrected problems per hour of review effort.[4] Participants become cynical about the value of the enterprise, leading to a downward spiral of program effectiveness.

Newer applications of the traditional approach seek to tighten the linkage between process criteria and patient outcomes. Criteria may be developed by consensus, but they are validated by studies that measure their association with the end results of care. Unfortunately, consensus development can be difficult and methodologies for achieving it are uncertain.[5] In addition, studies linking process to outcomes are expensive and correspondingly scarce.

Continuous Quality Improvement

The modern approach to quality assessment, Continuous Quality Improvement, is taken from industry. Industrial quality control procedures, which are linked to the improvements seen in Japanese products, seem to be effective. In their simplest form, as related to health care, these procedures consist of maintenance of control charts displaying the results of continuous sampling of patient care.

Few studies demonstrating the impact of Continuous Quality Improvement on patient outcomes have appeared in health services research journals. Nevertheless, two types of industrial quality control procedures have been used in health services: group process and statistical. While the group process approach, of which quality circles are perhaps the best known, entails the use of specialized studies and statistical analysis when needed, the bulk of the activity seems to revolve around group process. Slogans and posters are external evidence of a commitment to change employee attitudes about quality. Employee groups are formed to identify quality problems, study them, and recommend corrective action.

W. Edwards Deming's approach to quality control is sometimes confused with quality circles.[6] While Deming is no advocate of slogans and posters, he does insist that quality control charts be maintained at the production unit. The emphasis on the control chart is consistent with Deming's training as a statistician.

Continuous Quality Improvement in Health Services

Perhaps the best known application of Continuous Quality Improvement has been at the Harvard Community Health Plan.[7] Berwick and Knapp assert that learning from other industries will impress upon health care providers the importance of building quality into the patient care process ("quality by design"), broadening the concept of quality beyond the skillful delivery of efficacious care, and obtaining the commitment of senior managers to the quality control program.

Synthesis

By combining the strengths of the traditional Joint Commission on Accreditation of Healthcare Organizations approach[8] and the industrial approach, it is possible to develop a concept of quality assessment that is rational, cost-effective, and manageable. This preferred approach to quality assessment would have the following features:

- Routine reporting of aggregate data with interpretations provided by properly trained quality assessment staff. Reports would often be in the form of control charts based on Joint Commission indicators and other indicators that may be important locally.
- Use of pyramiding control charts for systematic exploration of deviations from expected values.
- Selection of clinically relevant indicators as continuous monitors. Such indicators may be specific to certain case types and should be standardized by epidemiological methods.
- Organization of quality assessment monitoring systems so that they support clinical managers.
- Expansion of the repertoire of corrective actions to include reallocating resources, reorganizing the flow of work, refining criteria for privileges, adjusting incentives for staff, and the like, rather than simply relying on continuing education.
- Avoidance of narrowly focused studies (e.g., studies of particular conditions or procedures) until analysis of aggregate data shows that they are needed.
- Avoidance of original data collection and focused audits unless they are absolutely necessary.

- Use in audits, whenever possible, of existing criteria taken from the clinical literature, thus avoiding the expense and bias of developing local standards. Practice guidelines developed by credible national bodies such as the Agency for Health Care Policy and Research should serve as the basis for criteria lists.
- Avoidance of efforts to develop new indicators until it is clear that they are essential. (Note: A discussion of newly developed indicators such as HEDIS is included in chapter 4.)

Development of a quality assessment program with these features will require commitment from top management, support from clinical leaders, and administrative expertise. While it seems odd that administrators are better trained in financial control methods than in quality control methods, it is nevertheless a fact that will make the design and operation of good quality assessment programs difficult. The solution may lie in the establishment of consortia of hospitals so that they may pool their resources and share quality assessment expertise. Alternatively, hospitals may purchase pyramiding control chart services from a vendor with several clients. Either approach would have the advantage of making possible comparisons of each client hospital's performance with that of peer hospitals. This would help to establish norms and thresholds and help hospitals interpret perturbations in quality indicators.

Monitoring Quality with Risk-Adjusted Indicators

Why Bother with Risk Adjustment?

Risk adjustment of quality assessment or utilization review surveillance data is an epidemiological technique that can be tricky but is sometimes essential and often useful.[9] For example, a control chart showing, as a performance indicator, the number of patients who returned to the emergency department after discharge might reveal a spike in September, causing the manager to suspect a problem. Before the manager could be sure a problem existed, however, it would be necessary to ask what, besides the quality of care, might cause fluctuations in the indicator. Clients may return to the emergency department for reasons unrelated to care the hospital provided. For example, some patients are discharged sicker than others simply because a longer period of recovery is required for some conditions. In short, a risk-adjusted rate might be more meaningful than simple frequency or even an unadjusted rate.

Risk adjustment is similar to case mix adjustment, severity adjustment, health status adjustment, and patient classification in that each of these procedures is used for the purpose of standardization, just as epidemiologists standardize death rates for differences in age distribution. Case mix adjustment, in its cruder forms, has simply consisted of using billing information to classify patients into groups that have similar costs. Severity adjustment was introduced to satisfy critics who charged that additional clinical differences among patients may cause legitimate differences in costs. Health status measures are often composed of items similar to those found in some severity indexes; therefore, health status adjustment is a population-level analog to severity adjustment. In short, case mix, severity, health status, and risk are all conceptually related in that they are just different varieties of standardization.

The Basic Approach

Six basic steps are followed in developing risk–adjusted monitors of outcomes or utilization. (This is a modified version of Blumberg's 10-step model.[10]) The procedure involves development of a statistical model and use of that model to adjust the data being monitored. The methods used are within the reach of managers who have had at least advanced training in statistics, including regression analysis.

Step 1: Select an indicator of quality. Most hospitals are now in the process of developing or borrowing performance indicators that can be routinely monitored (see Table 5.1 for examples). The validity of many of these indicators would be enhanced with risk adjustment.

Step 2: Identify candidate predictor variables. Consultation with clinicians is necessary to identify independent variables for inclusion in the risk model. Patient characteristics that are expected to be good predictors of the indicator should be selected

Table 5.1—Examples of Performance Indicators		
Type of Department	Outcomes	Utilization
Patient care	Mortality (unplanned) Complications Readmission Readmission to cardiac care unit Change in functional ability Return to operating room Nosocomial infections Incidents	Average length of stay Staff per patient Staff per patient day
Support	False positives Delays in reporting (e.g., lab test results, x-rays) Complaints Delays in obtaining beds	Ancillary services used per case (e.g., lab tests per case, x-rays per case) Staff per unit of output (e.g., staff per visit, staff per test, staff per report)

as variables. Unfortunately, much of the relevant clinical data will not be found in computerized databases.

Step 3: Obtain required data. The values of the indicators and the independent variables will be needed for each patient in the sample. For example, if the indicator is intensive care unit mortality and the independent variables are a severity score and patient age, then a data set will need to be constructed that contains severity and age for each patient and whether the patient lived or died.

Step 4: Estimate the equation. Indicators that are continuous variables (such as number of laboratory tests) can be modeled by means of ordinary least squares regression. Those that are nominal scale variables (such as death in the intensive care unit) can be predicted by means of logistic regression. Either procedure can be accomplished with a good spreadsheet program or a commercially available statistical package that works on a personal computer.

At this point, it may be discovered that the model does not work, meaning that the value of the performance indicator cannot be accurately predicted. If so, then the quality assessment program is no worse off than it was before developing the risk model; it can continue to monitor the indicator without adjustment for risk.

Step 5: Use the equation to predict the value of the indicator for each subsequent time period. Estimation of the equation gives coefficients that can be multiplied by the values of the independent variables, then summed, in each future time period. Let us say that actual deaths are increasing, which makes the death rate appear to be increasing. However, predicted deaths are increasing even faster, so risk adjusted mortality is declining. Either the standardized ratio or the difference can be charted as the new risk adjusted performance indicator.

Step 6: Update the model. The model may predict less well at some time in the future, as medical technology and the mix of cases change over time. Therefore, steps 1 through 4 should be repeated periodically.

Technical Issues

Attempts to develop risk-adjusted monitoring systems can be impeded by two technical issues: managerial problems related to implementation and methodological uncertainties. The latter can be expressed as follows:

- Can appropriate denominator data be defined and obtained?
- Should some indicators be monitored as frequencies rather than rates? This could be appropriate if even one occurrence of the event is unacceptable or if frequencies are too small.
- Are rare events too unstable to permit valid monitoring with control charts?
- Should control charts be monitored even if risk adjustment is not possible?
- Are chronological displays always best? Perhaps differences among units or product lines should be portrayed, rather than differences over time.
- Will analysis of aggregate data followed by focused audits fail to detect some problems? The existence of some problems may be

masked by aggregation. If so, supplementary problem identification systems may be required.

The Kaiser Permanente Case

HMOs have been studied extensively for several years. Wolinsky and Marder reviewed several studies of HMO performance and several reviews of the literature.[11] Although they found the results of these studies less than definitive, they were able to conclude that HMO performance was better than that of other health service delivery organizations in regard to hospitalization rates, total costs, use of preventive care, and client satisfaction with the technical aspects of care, but the process by which these results were achieved was unclear.

Building on Freidson's work,[12] Wolinsky and Marder hypothesized that HMOs perform better than other health service delivery organizations because they enjoy economies of scale, are more likely to engage in peer review, and are more likely to substitute support staff for physicians.[11] Furthermore, Wolinsky and Marder expected that independent practice associations would perform less well than staff or group model HMOs because they have the fewest organizational constraints and the weakest fiscal incentives; staff model HMOs would perform better because they have high organizational constraints, even though their physicians have weak fiscal incentives; and group model HMOs would perform best because they have both high organizational constraints and strong fiscal incentives. The authors further speculated that the Kaiser Permanente group model HMO would have the most bureaucratic controls and that this would significantly and positively affect the practice of medicine in that organization.

Staff and group model HMOs such as Kaiser Permanente are expected to use their organizational controls to minimize cost per enrollee, making them more efficient than HMOs of any other structural type. Quality is a different issue. While technical quality may increase directly with the degree of organizational control, what about the cost-effectiveness of care? The clinical efficiency of an organization can be catagorized as overtreatment, neutral treatment, and undertreatment.[13] Fee-for-service solo practitioners have an incentive to overtreat and they lack organizational controls to prevent this from happening. Capitated solo practitioners have an incentive to undertreat, which may be moderated in the group model because of the bureaucratic controls it offers. However, since staff and group model HMOs such as Kaiser Permanente also have bureaucratic controls and less fiscal incentive to undertreat, we would expect them to deliver the highest quality care. The staff model might be less successful than the group model at controlling costs, leading to care that is less cost-effective than that delivered by the group model.

This analysis does not lead to firm conclusions about the relative performance of different types of HMOs. However, there is reason to believe that HMOs of any type develop and implement bureaucratic controls more rapidly than solo practitioners or independent practice associations. Since Wolinsky and Marder expected group models to perform better than other types of HMOs, there was reason to make Kaiser Permanente the subject of a case study designed to address the following questions:[11] Did Kaiser Permanente achieve good performance (defined as cost-effective care for the enrolled population) because it has developed sophisticated control systems? And what were the control systems it used?

Interviews conducted at Kaiser Permanente in its Northwest Region in the late 1980s (as the boom in managed care was just beginning) did not lead to the expected findings. When asked how Kaiser Permanente achieved good performance, staff members gave answers that fell into three categories, relating to the structure, philosophy, and management of the organization.

Structure

Prepayment for care does not create incentives for inefficiency. Providers of fee-for-service care have an incentive to provide too much acute care—the more expensive the better—and too little preventive care. Fee-for-service providers are busy establishing coordination and control procedures to maximize their responsiveness to this incentive. Kaiser Permanente does not have to manage well to produce more cost-effective care; by not trying to deliver cost-ineffective care, it can easily outperform the fee-for-service system.

Physicians, the insurance plans, and the hospitals are integrated. Physicians are managed by physicians. The insurance plan owns the two regional Kaiser Permanente hospitals and a physician-administrator from the medical group and an administrator from the insurance plan are paired at each level of management. This ensures that both perspectives are voiced and results in close cooperation between the group and the plan. One reason given for the success of the dual structure is that getting physicians involved in administration causes them to become invested in organizational performance.

Furthermore, since Kaiser Permanente medical groups are for-profit groups, the physicians are acutely aware that their collective livelihood depends on efficient delivery of effective care. Established physicians retrain their newer colleagues to correct the inefficient practice styles that they were taught constituted "good medical care." The administrators, who are salaried staff in nonprofit hospitals, can afford to adopt a more noble stance. The effect is almost a reversal of roles, with the halo being handed to the administrator and the pitchfork to the physician.

A capped budget creates an incentive to plan carefully and avoid large, unexpected expenditures like no other budgetary arrangement. As it turns out, Kaiser Permanente hospitals are often very close to their expenditure targets at the end of the year. Even so, administrators are not satisfied with their precision, seeing much room for improvement and many missed opportunities. This attitude makes the organization receptive to innovations in coordination and control systems.

Philosophy

The plans see their members as populations or communities, while the physicians still see their patients as individuals. The population perspective enables administrators to plan for the long-term good of the community. At the same time, the physicians' focus on individual patients ensures that the needs of individuals do not become lost in the search for the greatest good for the greatest number. One result is that perhaps 75% of the care patients receive is indistinguishable from that delivered in the fee-for-service sector.

Success is not seen simply in terms of growth. Growth for its own sake seems to be a feature of fee-for-service medicine. Kaiser Permanente, on the other hand, does not particularly want to grow; growth means more work for the staff. Instead, staff would rather find ways to do their work more effectively and efficiently. However, growth has been a byproduct of good performance. For example, Kaiser Permanente has contracts with employers who must offer an HMO option to their employees. When more employees choose the Kaiser Permanente option, the number of enrollees increases.

Kaiser Permanente has a vision: It sees itself as delivering humane, effective care that is accessible and affordable. In the 1950s, 1960s, and 1970s, health administrators were generally not very effective. Many did not display leadership, functioning as clerks and "gofers" rather than pioneers. The popular view of the dynamic manager, akin to the gunslinger of the Old West, was false.

Kaiser Permanente was able to be more dynamic because its staff shared a vision. Interestingly, the organization never intended to deliver the cheapest care possible. Its objective was to make care accessible at a reasonable price, and when studies began to show how cost-effective its care was, even Kaiser Permanente was surprised.

Some informants suggested that the Kaiser Permanente vision has been key to its success. However, as the values of the larger society permeate the Kaiser Permanente system, performance may decline. One plan administrator went so far as to muse about encouraging Kaiser Permanente to establish its own health administration graduate program so that it can inculcate the proper values in its future managers.

Yet the organization does not strike its staff as being very ideological. Instead, it is characterized by its pragmatism and its "innocent commitment to community service."

Management

Changes in organization of care are triggered by a recognition of need for change on the part of physicians. Kaiser Permanente is characterized by its willingness to consider change. This openness has led to changes such as innovations in eye surgery (shifting to outpatient surgery improved patient outcomes), early involvement in hospice care as an alternative to intensive care for some patients, and establishment of committees to assist physicians as they address bioethical issues. These kinds of changes are championed by physician leaders and are not motivated by the desire to deliver more cost-effective care. Instead, creative members of the medical staff are simply seeking to test hypotheses about what works. Their conservative style of practice leads to innovation because they recognize that most medical care has never been proven effective in randomized trials. Therefore, the Kaiser Permanente physicians are free to experiment with conservative ways to deliver care, with conservative defined as biased against the risk of overtreatment.

Another explanation has been offered for Kaiser Permanente's tendency toward innovation: senior physicians become bored with the routines of patient care and want to experiment with reorganization "just for fun." If this is true, it is an interesting commentary about the practice of the noble profession of medicine.

Kaiser Permanente functions within the same malpractice environment that other health organizations must face. Therefore, it is limited in the degree to which it can innovate; it would be impossible to become too radical without facing legal action. However, the lack of a scientific basis for most medical practice leaves plenty of room for creativity.

Kaiser Permanente invests in people and research. The Kaiser Permanente hospitals in the Northwest have benefited from the research conducted by Kaiser Permanente's Center for Health Research, whose staff were described as the "original zealots" about effectiveness and efficiency of care. In addition, there are a program planning department in the regional office, which conducts efficiency studies; quality assessment departments in both regional hospitals; and a regional quality assessment office. There is also a regional quality assessment office in the Northern California region. This office faces a much different administrative challenge, because it seeks to monitor the performance of 20 hospitals instead of 2.

Besides investing in management research, Kaiser invests in its personnel, sending them to training programs around the nation.

Quality is monitored concurrently and utilization review is targeted at problem areas. At one Kaiser Permanente hospital, managers are asked to identify high-risk areas for the coming year. Only those few areas are monitored closely, with daily reports required by top management. An exhaustive review is completed on the high-risk areas at the end of the first quarter. If costs are higher than planned, specific causes of high costs are identified (e.g., the use of ventilators may be higher than usual). After the problem is identified, peer review of physicians' ordering patterns is triggered to determine whether any of the use of scarce resources is unnecessary.

Frills are trimmed if necessary to reduce costs. If costs exceed planned expenditures, hospitals in the Northwest Region consider generating needed savings by reducing the convenience of care to the subscriber. For example, waiting lists may be allowed to lengthen. Behind this strategy is the assumption that convenience is not a measure of quality; technical quality should not be allowed to suffer during periods of budgetary constraint.

Medical staff are actively managed. One of the first challenges faced by a new physician is the need to shed the bad habits learned in medical school. Arrogant types who are unwilling to conform to Kaiser Permanente's philosophy are not needed. Indeed, socialization of new physicians so that they will conform to the norms of the group may be one of the most powerful means by which the organization achieves good performance.

Hospital service chiefs are elected by the medical staff; however, there is a strong element of self-selection in this process because some doctors may refuse the honor. When they are strong, as they have been over most of Kaiser Permanente's history, service chiefs can lead the other physicians in a manner consistent with the organization's mission. Departmental managers in the medical groups, who are also elected, have formal authority over their fellow physicians, including the power to determine salary increases and bonuses. These managers push their staffs to become board certified, watch for obsolescence and burnout, and may restrict a physician's scope of practice for cause.

Chart review not only detects errors new physicians may be making, it also teaches them what the standards of practice actually are.   In fact, chart review for quality assurance is performed by the continuing education committee. The types of chart review conducted in the Kaiser Permanente system may be no more sophisticated than those performed elsewhere. One physician-manager insisted that this is true, but that chart review is more effective at Kaiser Permanente because Kaiser Permanente has an incentive to be serious about it.

Much of the review of clinical performance is accomplished informally. This is one of the benefits of a group practice environment; one informant described it as "the goldfish bowl effect." The Kaiser Permanente groups have been described as very collegial; this atmosphere might well be necessary for truly effective peer review. At the same time, the groups are described as more disciplined than some collegial organizations— university faculties, for instance. Sanctions may be imposed on physicians who perform poorly; however, these sanctions are often informal.

Specialists are selected carefully. The attitudes and behavior of the clinical specialists are key to medical management, not only because the services they order may be very expensive, but also because they are opinion leaders: their standards of practice become diffused throughout the organization. One physician-manager went so far as to say that specialists control the system and to assert that the system could best be controlled by limiting the number of specialists.

When Kaiser physicians report for work, they do so with the knowledge that the number of patients they must see is predetermined by the office staff; they cannot go home until they finish their lists. This system practically guarantees high productivity. It also has the advantage of giving doctors an incentive to become involved in chart review and administration: the work is easier.

When subscribers call for an appointment they are screened by telephone receptionists, who may refer them to an advice nurse. The advice nurse may advise subscribers that they do not need to see a physician. If subscribers do see primary care physicians, they are unlikely to be referred to specialists. Specialists also have heavy schedules and will not hesitate to complain if they receive unnecessary referrals.

While this system may appear to minimize use of physician time, it actually only controls it. Nurse practitioners or physician's assistants could be used more extensively, but interviewees said that early experiments did not reveal the use of paraprofessionals to be cost-effective. As the supply of physicians increased, it became even more sensible to use them for the first examination.

Conclusion

Kaiser Permanente illustrates just one type of managed care. The evolving structures of financial incentives and continuous quality improvement that characterize health care today diminish the relevance of the Kaiser Permanente example. For-profit managed care companies may have review systems that generate no clinically valid judgments about quality. In other ways, however, anecdotal evidence suggests that the quality advantage Kaiser Permanente once enjoyed over other forms of managed care may be diminishing as newer organizations improve their clinical management efforts. Nevertheless, undertstanding how Kaiser Permanente controlled quality at one point in history could give useful guidance to the planner who seeks to replicate that organization's success. Unfortunately, taken together, the explanations given above for Kaiser-Permanente's good performance clearly reveal that the organization's staff do not have a collective understanding of the reasons for their success.

One suspects that the process of medical management is not significantly more sophisticated at Kaiser Permanente than elsewhere in its use of technology and statistical monitoring techniques. The hypothesis that Kaiser Permanente would have the secret of medical management was not confirmed, unless the secret is pragmatic incrementalism coupled with a culture committed to a conservative practice style. Indeed, the evidence suggests that structure and norms arising from a clear vision about what constitutes good care have been more important than process in determining good performance.

Nevertheless, it is assumed that good management can enhance quality in most delivery systems, regardless of organizational culture. Good quality management will involve monitoring both process and outcomes of care. Efficient monitoring will start with aggregate data and, when problems are suspected, use more detailed data to focus on problems in particular physical locations, clinicians, or groups of clients.

It is in this step, the focused examination of suspected quality problems, that the traditional approach to quality assessment comes to the fore. Practice guidelines are used to develop lists of criteria. The care provided in individual cases is compared with the criteria. A score may be computed, such as the percentage of criteria met. These scores may be compared across office practices, hospitals, or other settings. Quality scores may be compared among different types of delivery systems, such as HMOs and preferred provider organizations. Ultimately, the decision about whether a particular type of delivery system should be emulated depends on its performance in meeting criteria that reflect a consensus of clinical judgments.

The community-oriented health planner is concerned about quality management because the planner is responsible for structuring the delivery system and monitoring the performance of provider organizations. Therefore, the planner will advise the governing board to insist on establishment of a quality management system and encourage them to ask for a review system that starts with aggregate data, followed, when necessary, by focused audits.

The planner's interest in appropriateness of care is motivated by concerns about both efficiency and quality. Managed care companies seeking to enroll local businesses and community residents are also motivated to control inappropriate overuse. However, managed care companies based outside the community may achieve savings by reduced benefits, cost sharing on the part of consumers, and micromanagement of patient care via a burdensome overlay of forms and required approvals. Therefore, the planner may choose to advise the local governing board that quality and efficiency can best be promoted by what might be called "self-managed care." Like Kaiser Permanente physicians, local physicians can assume risk and, through peer review rather than micromanagement, function in an accountable fashion.

REFERENCES

1. Donabedian A. *Explorations in Quality Assessment and Monitoring: I: The Definition of Quality and Approaches to Its Assessment.* Ann Arbor, Mich: Health Administration Press; 1980.
2. Rohrer JE. Monitoring the quality of health services. *Clinical Performance and Quality Health Care.* 1993;1(a):105–109.
3. Donabedian A. *A Guide to Medical Care Administration: II: Medical Care Appraisal —Quality and Utilization.* Washington, DC: American Public Health Association; 1969.
4. Rohrer JE. The secret of medical management. *Health Care Manage Rev.* 1989;14(3):7–13.
5. Chassin MR. Standards of care in medicine. *Inquiry.*1988;25:437–450.
6. Deming WE. *Out of the Crisis.* Cambridge, Mass: MIT Center for Advanced Engineering Study; 1986.
7. Berwick DM, Knapp MG. Theory and practice for measuring health care quality. *Health Care Financ Rev.* 1987;8 (suppl 1):49–55.
8. *The Joint Commission 1990 Accreditation Manual for Hospitals.* Chicago, Ill: Joint Commission on Accreditation of Healthcare Organizations; 1989.
9. Rohrer JE. Developing risk-adjusted monitoring systems: illustration of an approach. *Clinical Performance and Quality Health Care.* 1994;2(a):141–147.
10. Blumberg M. Risk adjusting health care outcomes: a methodologic review. *Med Care Rev.* 1986;43:351–393.
11. Wolinsky ED, Marder WD. *The Organization of Medical Practice and the Practice of Medicine.* Ann Arbor, Mich: Health Administration Press; 1985.
12. Freidson E. *Profession of Medicine: A Study of the Sociology of Applied Knowledge.* New York, NY: Harper & Row; 1970.
13. Rohrer JE. Managing for performance at Kaiser: health analytics or organization design. *Clinical Performance and Quality Health Care.* 1994;2(b):42–47.
14. Lord Dawson of Penn. *Interim Report on the future provisions of medical and allied services: United Kingdom Ministry of Health.* Consultative Council on Medical Allied Services. London: Her Majesty's Stationery Offices, 1920.

Chapter 6

Prospects and Training

██████ HE DEVELOPMENT OF SELF-MANAGED AND ACCOUNTABLE primary
██ ██ care systems is an exercise in local policy-making. This
██ ██ is an art about which little systematic information has
been collected. Yet, if development of local systems is
dependent on politics, then the planner must at least have
the benefit of the thoughts of some keen observers. For that
purpose, this section reviews some notions about the way
local health policy is formed. In the next section the other
fundamental obstacle to implementation of community-
oriented primary care systems—the training of health
system planners—is addressed.

The Politics of Local Health Policy

Study of a series of health care reform commissions in
New York City led Robert Alford to develop a theory about
power in a market economy.[1] He saw three groups vying for
control of the health care system. The first group, bureaucratic
reformers, sees hospitals as the centers of networks of clinics,
providing comprehensive care to local populations. This group
wants physicians and medical researchers to be subordinated to
the delivery system.

The second group, market reformers, has tended to see
competition among physicians and competition among
researchers as essential to efficiency. According to this perspective,
the delivery system is merely the framework which facilitates the
work of skilled professionals.[1]

Third, consumer groups offer another philosophy of
reform. If nonprofessionals are empowered, according to this
theory, the health care system will become more responsive and
more rational. However, consumer control seems to have been
achieved only rarely, and then only for short periods.

129

Reform by advocates of bureaucracy fails, according to Alford, because as the power of organized delivery systems increases, the systems become successful at garnering resources for their own ends. The market approach to reform also fails, because empowering health care professionals leads, obviously, to professional dominance, which in turn results in overinvestment in medical technology and generous reimbursement for those who employ it. In short, both types of reform are destroyed by their own success, since the empowered interests use opportunities created by reform to exploit resources from consumers, necessitating an additional round of reform.

Consumers can never win, according to Marmor and Morone , because they lack the resources to be as well organized as industry.[2] The regional health planning agencies established by federal legislation in 1974 (health systems agencies) were required to have consumer majorities on their boards. Nevertheless, provider interests tended to win out.

On the other hand, it is possible that provider victories were what consumers really wanted. Mick and Thompson examined public opinion data collected in 1978 and found little support for hospital cost containment.[3] Hospitals and doctors were perceived as having the public's interest at heart. Besides, consumers wanted their local hospitals to keep all their inpatient resources.

Health systems agencies were removed from the federal government's set of regulatory tools by the Reagan administration. States were allowed to continue the program if they were willing to provide funding. Some health systems agencies evolved into business coalitions; others simply went out of business. Interestingly, most states have certificate-of-need laws even today. The certificate of need was the main regulatory weapon of the health systems agencies.

Alford might have claimed that the evolution of health systems agencies proved that dynamics without change had once again been proven to characterize health care policy. A more straightforward interpretation of events might be that the more powerful economic interests (health care providers) got what they wanted, which was elimination of regulatory interference. Perhaps the certificate of need was retained (or reestablished) in many places because it allowed hospitals to restrict new entrants to local markets.

The changes in the medical market that are occurring now, resulting in the subjugation of health care providers to the cost-containment goals of major purchasers of care, would have been predicted by Alford's model if one has seen the major purchasers as allied with the largest hospitals and insurance companies. The goal of such bureaucratic reformers, once again, is to rationalize the market at the expense of the medical community. We might anticipate that consolidation of markets will eventually result in comfortable monopolies for the health care bureaucracies. Physicians will fight back with evidence of deteriorating quality of care. Consumers will join them. Another reform movement will commence, with the intention of wresting control from the corporations and passing it back to the other self-interested group, the medical community.

Does this mean that health care reform is hopeless? Not necessarily: a cyclical process contains plenty of room for optimism. After all, each reform movement results in correcting some of the deficiencies of the previous system. For a while, the new corrections coexist with the advantages left over from the old system. Eventually, deterioration occurs. The challenge lies in readjusting quickly enough to forestall deterioration.

For example, in the 1990s the pendulum is swinging toward curtailing investment in specialty care. The consumer can be expected to benefit from a reduced medical inflation rate. Eventually, however, bureaucracies will reduce specialty care too much, and access will suffer. The reform backlash will trigger new investment in medical care and reempowerment of physicians.

A well-managed local health care system would soften the impact of these swings of the pendulum. Cooperation among consumers, hospitals, physicians, and purchasers may achieve compromise positions acceptable to all. Monitoring accountability could detect deteriorating system performance early and allow for adjustments. The goal, therefore, is to substitute cooperative planning for political and economic warfare.

Given the nature of political economy in health care, what are the prospects for successful cooperative planning efforts?

This question can be seen as one relating to how the policy agenda is set at the local level. No matter that cooperative planning is extragovernmental rather than legislative; the process is inherently political.

The policy agenda literature tells us that policies are more likely to be adopted when (1) a problem or threat is widely recognized, (2) a potential solution to the problem is available, (3) a "policy entrepreneur" is willing to champion the solution, and (4) the solution does not run afoul of entrenched interests. This perspective suggests the following hypotheses regarding the adoption of local community health planning processes:

1.   Voluntary health planning is more likely to occur when there are serious problems in the local health system. Financial stress on the local medical care system could be such a trigger. Serious community health problems, such as high infant mortality, could also precipitate planning.
2.   Voluntary health planning is more likely to occur when a community leader steps forward to champion it.
3.   Voluntary health planning is more likely to occur in communities that have more resources to direct toward solving system problems.
4.   Voluntary health planning is more likely to occur when no single interest (such as the local hospital) has disproportionate economic (and thus political) power.

The above hypotheses are just that—no studies have verified them. Nevertheless, they serve to emphasize an important truth: Not all communities are likely to engage in community-oriented health planning. If and when they do, however, individuals trained in planning will be needed to contribute to the planning process. Where will such individuals come from?

Health Planning Education

Community health planning can be seen as a specialty in health services management. However, the capture of health services management by the ideology of competitive business is almost complete. At one time, health services administrators were custodians of the public interest; they recognized that their greatest responsibilities were to residents of the communities in which their organizations were located. The role of the administrator was to make sure health professionals had the resources they needed to do their jobs and to recruit and coordinate the health professionals required to meet community needs.

Those days seem to be well behind us. Every administrator recognizes that community needs cannot be met if the organization goes bankrupt. Therefore, the first responsibility of a good manager is to compete effectively. If any resources remain after the competitive battle has been fought, then unprofitable community services may be delivered. However, these services will be thought of as public relations efforts or perhaps as loss leaders. And such projects will have to compete with plans to add an atrium, install new carpeting, or put an attractive fountain in the lobby.

The health care system certainly has been commercialized. Managers are valued for their knowledge of financial management and marketing, not for their expertise in estimating how many health services are needed by defined populations. Yet the inadequacies of the priorities of the 1980s are becoming apparent. Excess hospital capacity has been rediscovered. Population-based planning may be reborn as well, as managed care seeks to size delivery systems to reduce utilization rates.

We start from the premise that health administration was oriented in a more appropriate direction before the 1980s, when competition became the overriding concern. The old approach to health administration did not have a name, because it was the only approach at the time. And after the business model achieved dominance it was unnecessary to give a name to the superseded approach.

From where we stand now, however, we can see two paths. The old public health model was giving rise to quantitative methods for use in community-oriented health planning. Then the development of analytical tools for population-based health planning was aborted when the business model took the field. By reviewing the development of health administration, we can chart what health planning might have become had health care management not become a business profession.

The Evolution of Health Administration

The earliest textbooks addressed hospital, not health, administration.[4] These books tended to focus on the detail of hospital structure and daily operations.[5,6] MacEachern's *Hospital Organization and Management*, for example, is thoroughly exhaustive about departmental operations.[6] Noticeably absent, however, are discussions of how the number of hospital beds required should be estimated or how the quality of patient care can be evaluated. It is perhaps partly in reaction to this lack that books taking an entirely different tack were published.

A 1965 text approaching health administration from a public health perspective was published by the American Public Health Association.[7] This brief volume by B. A. Myers, titled *A Guide to Medical Care Administration*, begins with a discussion of the medical care complex, which is composed of the individuals served by the medical care system, the professionals who provide services, and the organized arrangements that facilitate service delivery. The latter include health organizations such as hospitals, insurance companies, and regulatory agencies.

The most striking feature of the medical care complex is that it has a purpose: the delivery of good medical care, as defined in terms of accessibility, quality, continuity, and efficiency. By beginning with a statement of objectives, the text reveals the pristine rationality of its perspective. This feature requires emphasis, because rationality has gradually become displaced as the dominant approach to health administration.[4] The pursuit of lucrative markets is not the same as addressing the most serious health needs of the community.

A second striking feature of the text is its use of the term "medical care." Instead of medical care administration, we now say health services administration, health administration, health care administration, or health care management. The change in terminology reflects a broader role for the health administrator and also a generation of attacks on the "medical model," which has been criticized as emphasizing treatment over prevention.[4] However, the change has been largely cosmetic, since most of the health services system is still oriented toward medical treatment.

The change in terminology does not invalidate Myers' perspective; other grounds will have to be found.

The second part of Myers' book addresses what she calls the principles of medical care administration. Medical care programs have objectives that are consistent with the purpose of medical care and the needs of the community, and they have structures and functions consistent with the achievement of those objectives. Medical care administration is the process of integrating those objectives, structures, and functions. Integration is accomplished by planning, management, and evaluation, each equal in importance, according to Myers.

Of course, there has always been a chief executive officer (CEO) who is ultimately responsible for all three functions; in this sense, planning is subordinate to management. However, at one level below the CEO planning can be seen as at least coequal with day-to-day management. In large organizations an obvious distinction between planners and managers may appear: planners are staff, whereas managers have line responsibilities. Despite this difference in formal authority, planners may be as influential as managers or more so if the CEO values their concerns and recommendations.[4]

Planning involves the description of health needs and resources available, the analysis of these data, the evaluation of alternatives (how the most can be accomplished with the limited resources available), and the definition of program goals, structure, and functions that will meet population needs. According to Myers, planning guides management, rather than the reverse.

Mid level management takes place within the structures determined by planners. It is predicated on the objectives identified by planners, and it executes the functions deemed necessary by planners. It focuses on documentation, development, and maintenance of internal and external relationships; development and maintenance of standards of quality and quantity; and control of resource use to ensure efficiency.[4] The technical functions of quality assurance and maintenance of efficiency each carry as much weight as the more interpersonal functions of internal and external coordination. Indeed, the second and larger volume of *A Guide to Medical Care Administration* deals exclusively with the appraisal of quality, which reflects the importance of quality relative to the more generic management activities.[8]

In Myers' formulation, program evaluation provides constant feedback to planners. The degree to which goals are met may suggest revision of program structure and functions or modification of the goals themselves. Evaluation, like planning and maintenance of standards, should be accomplished in a rational-comprehensive, objective fashion.

The rational public health approach to health administration was continued in Donabedian's *Aspects of Medical Care Administration* in 1973.[9] The stated purpose of the book is to address three major tasks faced by health administrators: (1) definition of objectives, (2) assessment of needs for services, and (3) assessment of the adequacy of health resources. The approach is indeed systematic and offers a planning-oriented perspective on health administration that integrates all disciplines. However, it does not address the interpersonal aspects of management or the manager's coordination role.

Viewed from the vantage point of health administration in the 1990s, it is fascinating that Donabedian's text was characterized as addressing administration rather than simply planning. It reflects the reality that at least some of the experts at the apex of the field regarded teaching the analytics of planning as more important than teaching the interpersonal, qualitative, or generic business aspects of management. Many practitioners and academics believed that while these subjects were important, most managers, given the aptitude, could pick up the techniques through a combination of experience and a general course or two. The important educational deficit, and one that could not be corrected without the aid of formal training, was in the sphere of health care analysis.[4] A manager with a general business background and good interpersonal skills who lacked guidance from a competent health analyst would be unlikely to achieve the objectives of the medical care system. Furthermore, a narrow knowledge of quantitative techniques was insufficient. The administrator needed to make decisions based on techniques fully in tune with the unique characteristics of health services and reflecting an awareness of the interdependencies in the system. Most important, the administrator should operate with a model of the community health system in his or her mind, for the purposes of organizing data and adhering to the objectives of the health system.

Although *Aspects* might be characterized as a planning text, it differs greatly from other books on health planning.[10-12] Sophisticated quantitative techniques are included in some of these books, as are qualitative methods. Indeed, some focus almost entirely on the political aspects of areawide planning; others are organized around strategic planning, which is sometimes taken as an excuse for offering the most marketable services rather than those most needed.

Aspects is analytical in a nonquantitative sense: it disassembles the health system to reveal the working parts, then offers models clarifying interrelationships. That no single manager has control over the health system is obvious, but this fact does not eliminate the need for the manager to perform administrative tasks such as planning and evaluation. This perspective on health administration naturally lends itself to the production of health policy analysts, HMO administrators, and Blue Cross executives as well as hospital administrators.

An entirely different perspective is introduced in Levey and Loomba's *Health Care Administration: A Managerial Perspective*, published in the same year as Donabedian's *Aspects*.[13] This text is notable for three reasons: (1) At the outset it stresses the conflict between the growing demand for health services and constraints on supply, and it argues that more could be squeezed out of existing resources with modern (in 1973) management. (2) It unequivocally establishes planning and evaluation as dimensions of management. (3) It introduces the perspective that there is a field called management that includes health management, whether managers of health organizations know it or not, and it pointedly asserts that health care managers could learn a great deal from the non-health (business) management literature.

Levey and Loomba's text is similar to *Aspects* in that it adopts a rational-comprehensive perspective. It devotes a chapter to systems analysis; a chapter to planning, programming, and budgeting; and three chapters to management science. However, instead of being organized around the objectives of the health system, it reflects the various functions of management (for example, decision making, planning, evaluation, and control).

The second edition of Levey and Loomba's text is even more managerial in thrust.[14] For example, planning has been recast as operations planning. The book focuses explicitly on what can be learned from strategic planning in business rather than on the techniques of health planning. In addition, the revised edition introduces a note of heresy: It gives more space to the perspective that rational-comprehensive approaches may not be very workable. For example, even though planning is defined as objective and rational, the text also says that planning *may* be formal and *may* be supported by conscious or deliberate efforts (p. 241, emphasis added). The reader must conclude that informal, unconscious, accidental planning is still planning. Indeed, this is consistent with the observation that people are not fully rational and that "muddling through" is the norm rather than the exception.[15] Furthermore, the text asserts, rational-comprehensive planning cannot succeed where problems are ill defined or unquantifiable.

Two approaches to health administration can be discerned from the preceding discussion.[4] One, which we might call traditional health administration, emphasizes analytical techniques that are specific to health services and focuses on meeting community health needs. The second approach emphasizes the application of business management techniques to health services. Furthermore, it parallels trends in business management in that it has begun to stress the qualitative aspects of management at least as much as quantitative skills. The two approaches can perhaps be contrasted best by exposing what each undervalues almost to the point of exclusion. The traditional approach, as has already been noted, does not deal with the coordination role of health administrators. The managerial approach does not conceive of a general health care manager; the manager is a generalist in handling people or a specialist in the application of one of a narrow set of business techniques to health services.

Levey and Loomba's perspective on health administration proved to be more popular than Donabedian's. At the time *Aspects* was published, a bifurcation already was occurring in course materials. While general health administration texts emphasized management over specialized health care management techniques, supplementary textbooks covered techniques for planning and evaluation that are tailored for health services.[16,17] Griffith's *Cost-Control in Hospitals, Quantitative Techniques for Hospital Planning and Control,* and *Measuring Hospital Performance* contain formulas and analytical procedures that reflect their origins.[18-20] Many were developed in hospitals; some were borrowed from other fields but refined for application to health services. They do not simply represent the undigested application of general business techniques. It was not long, however, before it became common to apply to health administration techniques developed elsewhere, with little modification. Forecasting techniques developed in business were applied to health services; indeed, the whole notion of planning became wedded to the foreign concept of marketing.[21] Evaluation of health services rapidly began to look like evaluation research in general, although quality assurance remained relatively unaffected until the late 1980s.[22,23] The marriage of marketing and planning is perhaps most surprising. Griffith assumed that if a hospital offered services needed by the community it would do well, and if it offered unneeded services it would do poorly. This assumption contrasts sharply with the familiar litany of health administration with a public health bent: that need does not equal demand because the consumer is not rational, fully informed, or able to plan needed purchases. Furthermore, need for care is frequently accompanied by inability to pay.

The Traditional Perspective
in Health Administration

As it appears in retrospect from a perusal of texts, the perspective that has faded from health administration has the following characteristics:[4]

1. It is oriented toward meeting community needs and thus is inherently epidemiological, as befits its public health origins. More specifically, it seeks to meet as many health needs as possible with limited resources.

2. It assumes that need for medical services can be estimated

quantitatively and that the performance of medical care providers in meeting those needs can be measured.

3.   It recognizes that accurate estimates of medical care needs and evaluation of system performance in meeting those needs require use of epidemiological methods (e.g., location of disease in person, place, and time; standardization of rates) and an understanding of the unique characteristics of medical care (e.g., the centrality of the patient-provider relationship, the differing perspectives of clients and providers, and the relevance of biology and physiology to the production process).

4.   It is rational-comprehensive, meaning that it seeks to take into account all important factors and lead to decisions that will optimize objectives. Of course, it is never possible to include all factors in the analysis of a problem. Nevertheless, an effort can be made to capture most of them.

5.   It regards the analytic challenge as more important and more scholarly than the coordination chores involved in management.

Analytic methods used in health administration to plan and evaluate medical care must take into account clinical realities. This body of techniques is distinct from any methods that can be derived independently of medicine and public health. Health care analysts need not be clinicians if they are trained to use approaches that automatically respond to clinical realities. It is likely, however, that most advances in analytic methods will come from clinicians who are cross-trained in planning and evaluation. Operations management techniques developed in business can be useful tools in the armamentarium of health analysts, but such techniques have to be carefully modified in application to reflect clinical realities. A single example illustrates this point: time–series methods can be used to forecast hospital utilization. However, planners must recognize that hospital utilization fluctuates for biological reasons, such as the number of women of childbearing age, seasonal epidemics, and morbidity arising from poor food or living conditions. The business analyst could not develop reasonable models for forecasting hospital utilization without indoctrination in relevant clinical considerations. In the end, the analytic techniques used by the analyst might be dramatically different from what he or she learned in business school.

What Went Wrong?

The development of analytic methods specialized for health administrators seems to have been aborted. The public health perspective is less visible in health administration today, and the population-based planning techniques under development in the 1970s are no longer taught in many graduate programs. Many do not offer a class in health planning. In short, it appears that the development of health planning techniques came to a halt a generation ago.

Several factors may have contributed to the diversion of the major health administration programs away from production of community-oriented health planners. These include (1) the increasing pressure on health administrators to avoid negative net revenue; (2) a generation of federal policy emphasizing an antiplanning, market ideology in health care; and (3) widespread cynicism about what rational-comprehensive approaches to decision making can actually accomplish. Of these factors, perhaps the change of values from community service to revenue generation is the most important.

On the other hand, perhaps the most important reason health planning methods fell out of favor was failure to give them a fair test. Most administrators practicing in the 1970s, when the techniques were in their formative stages, never learned them well enough to use them to advantage. Health administration programs taught courses in these techniques, but it is not clear that students understood what was being offered. And the techniques themselves required additional refinement. It would be fair to say that few nonfinancial advances in health analytic techniques have found their way into the classroom since the 1970s.

The failure to improve health planning methods can be attributed, at least partially, to the disciplinary organization of health services research. Each of the disciplines is burdened with its own assumptions about appropriate methods and how knowledge can be acquired. Some researchers constantly compare data with theory and others dredge through data in search of testable hypotheses. Some researchers are convinced that only the perceptions of patients and health professionals are worth analyzing; others insist on hard data.[24]

While researchers squabble over such issues, our ability to estimate requirements for health resources and to evaluate system performance remains underdeveloped. If researchers would remember that they share a common objective—guiding the health system toward maximum effectiveness with limited resources—then perhaps progress could once again be made. Epidemiology is the only discipline fully open to the perspectives of others, as is proven by its acceptance of the importance of social factors as determinants of disease. Until the epidemiological attitude becomes more prevalent, the primitive analytic methods now available for planning must be preserved and communicated to practitioners. At this point, it seems that the best hope for methodological innovation will come from the field, where managers have little time to devote to philosophical irrelevancies.

Conclusion

Who are the health planners of the future? Who would benefit from reading this book? What kinds of university programs should train health planners? At one time health planning fell naturally into the domain of health care management programs. Now, an objective assessment would conclude that many health administration programs have drifted away from the subject and that anyone who wishes to learn the methods can enter the field. There is no apparent reason why nurses, social workers, policy analysts, regional planners, community developers, public administrators, and public health administrators cannot play important roles in community health planning. All that is needed is a community-oriented perspective, some background knowledge about health and health care, and command of basic techniques.

More specifically, the following recommendations can be advanced about health planning education.

1. Target people who intend to pursue careers in state or local public health administration, nursing, management of primary care delivery systems, or community development. The degrees they

currently possess and the specific degree programs in which they are enrolled are less important than career objectives.

2. As a corollary to the above, health planning education does not have to lead to granting of a specialized degree in health planning. Planning programs could teach electives or packages of electives in a variety of degree programs.

3. As a corollary to points 1 and 2, it is clear that the specific set of courses planning students should be exposed to will vary depending on the content of the core curriculum in their own degree programs. Students in a master of public health degree program will be required to learn about epidemiology, statistics, computer methods, health behavior, environmental health, and health policy. To become equipped to function as planners they will need to pick up some health economics, management theory, management research methods such as quality improvement, and, of course, a planning course that uses a book such as this one. Students will need to conduct a planning project in the field and practice public speaking and working in small groups.

Students in the fields of regional planning and community development will have public speaking, small group skills, computer methods, statistics, research methods, economics, and possibly management theory as part of their core curriculum. Epidemiology, health behavior, environmental health, health policy and health planning will need to be added. Business management students will need similar courses. Nursing administration and community health nursing students will also need customized sets of electives to become competent at planning.

4. The depth the student needs in each subject will also depend on his or her career objectives. A state health planner may need a better grasp of how to calculate resource requirements, whereas a local public health administrator or manager of a primary care system may need more general management skills. One might expect (or at least hope) that career opportunities for well-trained health planners will expand as state governments become more deeply involved in oversight of managed care organizations. At the local level, we might anticipate an increase in interest among clinicians in training that will enable them to manage primary care delivery systems. For this reason, physicians and nurses might be early registrants for population-oriented health care management and planning courses.

This book introduces the reader to basic health planning methods approached from an epidemiological, or population-based, perspective. In the final analysis, all truly useful management techniques are simple in application. If the reader is now confident that he or she can appropriately employ the methods presented, then the effort can be counted as an unqualified success for all parties.

Turning fragmented local delivery systems into coordinated primary care systems will be difficult. This challenge constitutes nothing less than developing the health care delivery system of the future. Despite its difficulty, however, such development is a necessary strategic move for local providers.

It is also an excellent way for providers to discharge their civic responsibility to function as community leaders. In the 1980s, leadership seemed to have an individualistic definition. Effective leaders leaped into the competitive fray and changed their organizations by force of will, charisma, and good management. In the 1990s, leaders are empowering their workers; they lead from behind. In the year 2000, leaders will need to step even further back. Empowering communities means giving up control over future directions. Influence remains, but accountability moderates its force. This ceding of control takes courage, but the traditional value system of the field of health administration supports it.

Unfortunately, good intentions and skill together may not be sufficient to empower communities to govern their health care systems. Lawrence Brown and Catherine McLaughlin evaluated Community Programs for Affordable Health Care, a group of projects funded by the Robert Wood Johnson Foundation, to demonstrate the potential of effective cooperation at the local level.[25] Brown and McLaughlin concluded that community leaders would not be likely to organize themselves into stable negotiating structures able to exercise economic discipline. Health care is big business at the local level, health care professionals have great influence, and no simple solution to the problems of access, cost, and quality presents itself. Most importantly, the causes of inflation are not at the community level, but instead in state and federal programs, insurance company board rooms, and regional health system headquarters.

Not everyone agrees. Robert Sigmond has articulated a powerful argument in favor of communities' control over and coordination of their health care systems.[26] Walter McNerney and Phillip Newbold have also written about the importance of community-based initiatives.[27,28] Perhaps the fundamental point to be made about feasibility is that community-based health systems management is possible, given dynamic local leadership and a shared commitment to quality of life. Success is by no means guaranteed, however, and that, in a nutshell, is the challenge facing community health planners.

REFERENCES

1. Alford RR. *Health Politics: Dynamics without Change*. Chicago, Ill: University of Chicago Press; 1976.
2. Marmor TR, Morone JA. Representing consumer interests: imbalanced markets, health planning, and the HSAs. *Milbank Mem Fund Q Health Soc*. 1980;58:125–165.
3. Mick SS, Thompson JD. Public attitudes toward health planning under the health systems agencies. *J Health Polit Policy Law*. 1984;8:782–800.
4. Rohrer JE. Health analytics: the road not traveled. *J Health Adm Educ*. 1989;7(2):230–243.
5. McGibony JR. *Principles of Hospital Administration*. New York, NY: GP Putnam's Sons; 1952.
6. MacEachern MT. *Hospital Organization and Management*. Chicago, Ill: Physician's Record Company; 1935.
7. Myers BA. *A Guide to Medical Care Administration: I: Concepts and Principles*. Washington, DC: American Public Health Association; 1965.
8. Donabedian A. *A Guide to Medical Care Administration: II: Medical Care Appraisal — Quality and Utilization*. Washington, DC: American Public Health Association; 1969.
9. Donabedian A. *Aspects of Medical Care Administration*. Cambridge, Mass: Harvard University Press; 1973.
10. Nutt PC. *Planning Methods for Health and Related Organizations*. New York, NY: John Wiley & Sons Inc; 1984.
11. Blum HL. *Planning for Health: Generics for the Eighties*. 2nd ed. New York, NY: Human Sciences Press; 1981.
12. Hyman HH. *Health Planning: A Systematic Approach*. Germantown, Md: Aspen; 1976.
13. Levey S, Loomba NP. *Health Care Administration: A Managerial Perspective*. Philadelphia, Pa: J.B. Lippincott; 1973.
14. Levey S, Loomba NP. *Health Care Adminstration: A Managerial Perspective*. 2nd ed. Philadelphia, Pa: J.B. Lippincott; 1984.
15. Lindblom CE. The science of muddling through. *Public Adm Rev*. 1959;19 (Spring):79–88.
16. Bergwall DV, Reeves PN, Woodside NB. *Introduction to Health Planning*. 2nd ed. Washington, DC: Information Resources Press; 1979.

17. MacStravic RS. *Determining Health Needs.* Ann Arbor, Mich: Health Administration Press; 1978.
18. Griffith JR, Hancock WM, Munson FC, eds. *Cost Control in Hospitals.* Ann Arbor, Mich: Health Administration Press; 1976.
19. Griffith JR. *Quantitative Techniques for Hospital Planning and Control.* Lexington, Mass: DC Heath and Co; 1972.
20. Griffith JR. *Measuring Hospital Performance.* Chicago, Ill: Blue Cross Association; 1978.
21. Griffith JR. *The Well-Managed Community Hospital.* Ann Arbor, Mich: Health Administration Press; 1987.
22. Veney JE, Kaluzny AD. *Evaluation and Decision Making for Health Services Programs.* Englewood Cliffs, NJ: Prentice-Hall; 1984.
23. Nutt PC. *Evaluation Concepts and Methods: Shaping Policy for the Health Administrator.* Jamaica, NY: Spectrum Publications; 1981.
24. Rohrer JE. Philosophy of science and health services research: a cross-disciplinary critique and call for action. *J Health Adm Educ.* 1989;7: 543–556.
25. Brown LD, McLaughlin C. Constraining costs at the community level: a critique. *Health Aff. (Millwood);* Winter 1990:5–46.
26. Sigmond RM. Collaboration in a competitive environment: the pursuit of community health. *Front Health Serv Manage.* 1995;11:5–36.
27. McNerney WJ. Community health initiatives are widespread, challenging our sense of civic obligation. *Front Health Serv Manage.* 1995;11:39–44.
28. Newbold PA. Building healthy communities. *Front Health Serv Manage.* 1995;11:45–48.

Appendix

This appendix contains a questionnaire developed by the Health of the Public project at the University of Iowa. The Health of the Public project was funded by the Pew and Robert Wood Johnson foundations to stimulate progressive changes in academic medical centers. The Iowa effort included a partnership with the North Iowa Mercy Medical Center to conduct health system development projects in rural communities. The questionnaire is intended to serve as a model for other communities. In practice, we might expect planning groups to edit it to reflect local concerns.

HOWARD COUNTY
HEALTH CARE ADVISORY GROUP
HEALTH ASSESSMENT SURVEY

PART I. QUESTIONS PERTAINING TO YOUR
COMMUNITY'S HEALTH

In your opinion, how much of a problem is each of these issues in Howard County? No problem? Minor problem? Major problem? Or do you feel you don't know enough about a particular problem to determine whether it's a problem or not? Please express your opinion by checking the appropriate column.

Health Problem	No Problem	Minor Problem	Major Problem	Don't Know
Babies born underweight or premature	❑	❑	❑	❑
Birth defects	❑	❑	❑	❑
Pregnancy care for low-income women	❑	❑	❑	❑
Unplanned pregnancy	❑	❑	❑	❑
Teen pregnancy	❑	❑	❑	❑
Sexually transmitted diseases (syphillis, gonorrhea, HIV/AIDS)	❑	❑	❑	❑
Alcohol abuse or drug abuse	❑	❑	❑	❑
Smoking/tobacco use	❑	❑	❑	❑
Nutrition (eating healthy foods)	❑	❑	❑	❑
Lack of physical activity and fitness	❑	❑	❑	❑
Problems with teeth or gums	❑	❑	❑	❑
Cancer	❑	❑	❑	❑
Heart disease	❑	❑	❑	❑
Diabetes	❑	❑	❑	❑
Diseases of the elderly (arthritis, stroke, Alzheimer's disease)	❑	❑	❑	❑
Depression/suicide	❑	❑	❑	❑
Access to emergency medical services	❑	❑	❑	❑
Access to specialty health care	❑	❑	❑	❑
Adequate housing	❑	❑	❑	❑

Health Problem	No Problem	Minor Problem	Major Problem	Don't Know

Access to primary (family physician) health care

1. For low-income children	❑	❑	❑	❑
2. For the elderly	❑	❑	❑	❑
3. For all in community	❑	❑	❑	❑

Violence

1. Murder	❑	❑	❑	❑
2. Sexual assault	❑	❑	❑	❑
3. Child abuse/neglect	❑	❑	❑	❑
4. Elder abuse/neglect	❑	❑	❑	❑
5. Beatings between young adults	❑	❑	❑	❑
6. Spouse/partner beating	❑	❑	❑	❑
7. Workplace violence	❑	❑	❑	❑
8. Gangs	❑	❑	❑	❑

Injuries

1. Motor vehicle	❑	❑	❑	❑
2. Farm	❑	❑	❑	❑
3. Work-related	❑	❑	❑	❑
4. Burns	❑	❑	❑	❑
5. Drowning	❑	❑	❑	❑
6. Home	❑	❑	❑	❑
7. Sports	❑	❑	❑	❑
8. Firearms	❑	❑	❑	❑

Environmental exposures

1. Air pollution	❑	❑	❑	❑
2. Water pollution	❑	❑	❑	❑
3. Radon	❑	❑	❑	❑
4. Toxic exposures at work	❑	❑	❑	❑
5. Toxic exposures at home	❑	❑	❑	❑
6. Food poisoning	❑	❑	❑	❑
7. Drug safety	❑	❑	❑	❑

Any other health problems?

_____

_____

_____

PART II. HEALTH CARE SERVICES

1. Please answer the following questions in the chart below.

   a. In the last 12 months which of the following services have <u>you or a member of your household</u> used? *Place a check mark for services used in column A below.*

   b. In the last 12 months which of these services have <u>you or a member of your household</u> used <u>outside</u> of Howard County? *Please make a check mark for services used in column B below.*

   c. In the last 12 months, for services in Howard County, were <u>you or a member of your household</u> satisfied with the quality of services received? *Circle Y for yes, N for no in column C below.*

   d. In the last 12 months was the distance <u>you or a member of your household</u> had to travel for services reasonable? *Circle Y for yes, N for no in column D below.*

   e. In the last 12 months did <u>you or a member of your household</u> find the cost of the services to be reasonable? *Circle Y for yes, N for no in column E below.*

	Used Service	Outside County	Quality Satisfactory		Distance Reasonable		Reasonable Cost	
	A	**B**	**C**		**D**		**E**	
Physicians			Y	N	Y	N	Y	N
Physician assistants			Y	N	Y	N	Y	N
Hospitals			Y	N	Y	N	Y	N
Nursing homes			Y	N	Y	N	Y	N
Pharmacies			Y	N	Y	N	Y	N
Emergency medical services			Y	N	Y	N	Y	N
Dentists			Y	N	Y	N	Y	N
Homemaker services			Y	N	✕		Y	N
Home health nursing services			Y	N	✕		Y	N
Physical therapy services			Y	N	Y	N	Y	N
Eye care			Y	N	Y	N	Y	N
Counseling and/or mental health care			Y	N	Y	N	Y	N
Alcohol and/or drug treatment			Y	N	Y	N	Y	N
Chiropractors			Y	N	Y	N	Y	N

2.   In the last 12 months, when you wanted to be seen as soon as possible, did you have to wait more than 3 days for an appointment to see a doctor for primary (not specialty) health care? *Circle one.*
        a. Yes   b. No   c. Does not apply   d. Don't know

3.   In the last 12 months, did you have to wait more than 15 minutes in the doctor's waiting room for primary (not specialty) health care? *Circle one.*
        a. Yes   b. No   c. Does not apply   d.Don't know

4.   Was your medical care kept private (confidential)? *Circle one.*
        a. Yes   b. No   (Please see 4A)   c. Does not apply
        d. Don't know
        4A.Who do you feel is responsible for the lack of confidentiality?
              1. Physician   2. Office staff   3. Hospital staff
              4. Other _____

5.   Does a feeling of community loyalty influence your decision to seek services inside Howard County? *Circle one.*

        a. Yes   b. No   c. Don't know

6.   Do you feel that the following services in Howard County need improvement?
        Circle Yes, No, or Does not apply for each item.

a.	Transportation (regional or senior transit)	Yes	No	Does not apply
b.	Hospice	Yes	No	Does not apply
c.	Farm safety education (adult and child)	Yes	No	Does not apply
d.	Elderly (geriatric) services (If yes, please specify type of service)	Yes	No	Does not apply
e.	Meals on wheels	Yes	No	Does not apply
f.	Home care	Yes	No	Does not apply
g.	Emergency ambulance service	Yes	No	Does not apply
h.	Support systems (If yes, please specify type of system)	Yes	No	Does not apply
i.	Preventive programs (If yes, please specify type of program)	Yes	No	Does not apply
j.	Public health	Yes	No	Does not apply
k.	Child care (If yes, circle items that apply)	Yes	No	Does not apply

              (1) Before/after school
              (2) Preschool
              (3) Other (specify) _____

        l.   Any other services? _____

7.   If you or a family member needed to enter a nursing home, which one would you prefer to enter? *Circle one.*
     a.   Evans Memorial Home
     b.   Howard County Residential Care Facility
     c.   Patty Elwood Center
     d.   Cresco Care Center
     e.   Colonial Manor
     f.   Riceville Rest Home
     g.   Other

8.   How many times have <u>you</u> seen a physician during the past 12 months? _____

9.   In the last 12 months, how many times were <u>you or a member of your household</u> an inpatient or outpatient (includes x-ray, lab, etc.) at Howard County Hospital? _____

10.   Were <u>you or a member of your household</u> admitted to a hospital other than Howard County Hospital in the last 12 months?

     a.   Yes   If yes, list hospital(s) and location(s):
     1. _____
     2. _____
     b.   No

11.   Do you have any kind of health care coverage, including health insurance, prepaid plans such as HMOs (health maintenance organizations), or government plans such as Medicare? *Circle one.*
     a.   Yes (Go to questions 12 and 13)
     b.   No (Go to Question 14)
     c.   Don't know/not sure

If you do have health coverage:
12.   What kind of health care coverage do you have? *Circle all that apply.*
     a.   Private pay (you pay all expenses)
     b.   Individual/family /group insurance (If so, who pays your premium? Please check one. ____ self ____ employer ____ shared)
     c.   Medicare (Social Security)
     d.   Medicaid (Title 19)
     e.   VA
     f.   Dental insurance
     g.   Other _____

13.   Does your health insurance adequately cover the cost of your health care? *Circle one.*   a. Yes   b. No   (Go to question 15)

If you do not have health care coverage:

14. About how long has it been since you had health care coverage?
       Circle one.
       a. Within the past 6 months (1 to 6 months ago)
       b. Within the past year (6 to 12 months ago)
       c. Within the past 2 years (1 to 2 years ago)
       d. Within the past 5 years (2 to 5 years ago)
       e. 5 or more years ago
       f. Don't know/not sure
       g. Never

15. Was there a time during the last 12 months when <u>you</u> needed to see
       a doctor, but could not because of the cost? *Circle one.*
       a. Yes
       b. No
       c. Does not apply
       d. Don't know/not sure

16. About how long has it been since <u>you</u> last visited a doctor for a
       routine checkup? *Circle one.*
       a. Within the past year (1 to 12 months ago)
       b. Within the past 2 years (1 to 2 years ago)
       c. Within the past 5 years (2 to 5 years ago)
       d. 5 or more years ago
       e. Don't know/not sure
       f. Never

17. In the last 30 days, how much out-of-pocket money (not covered
       by any form of insurance) have <u>you</u> spent for prescription and
       over-the-counter drugs? *Circle one.*
       a. $0-$10
       b. $11-$50
       c. $51-$100
       d. $101-$200
       e. Over $200

18. Was there a time during the last 12 months when <u>you</u> needed to
       buy prescription drugs, but could not because of cost? *Circle one.*
       a. Yes
       b. No
       c. Does not apply
       d. Don't know/not sure

PART III. HEALTH BEHAVIOR

1. Do you use seat belts when you travel? *Circle one.*
   a. Never
   b. Sometimes
   c. Always
   d. Only on the highway

2. Do your children use seat belts/restraints? *Circle one.*
   a. Never
   b. Sometimes
   c. Always
   d. Does not apply

3. During the past month, did you participate (on or off your job) in any physical activities or exercise such as running, calisthenics, golf, gardening, or walking? *Circle one.*
   a. Yes (Go to questions 4 and 5)
   b. No (Go to question 6)
   c. Don't know/not sure (Go to question 6)

If yes:

4. How many times per week or per month did you take part in this activity? *Circle one/fill in blank.*
   a. Times per week _____
   b. Times per month _____
   c. Don't know/not sure

5. When you took part in this activity, how many minutes or hours did you usually keep at it? *Circle one/fill in blank.*
   a. Hours/minutes ___ / ___ ___
   b. Don't know/not sure

6. How much alcohol do you drink? *Circle one.*
   a. None
   b. One or less each week (bottle/can of beer, glass of wine, or mixed drink)
   c. Less than one each day
   d. One or two each day
   e. More than two each day

7.   Do you wear a protective helmet when you ride a motorcycle?
        Circle one.
        a.   Never
        b.   Sometimes
        c.   Always
        d.   Does not apply

8.   Do you and your child(ren) wear protective helmets when you ride
        bicycles? *Circle one.*
        a.   Never
        b.   Sometimes
        c.   Always
        d.   Does not apply

9.   Have you smoked at least 100 cigarettes in your entire life? *Circle
        one.*
        a. Yes   b. No   c. Don't know/not sure

10.   Do you smoke cigarettes now? *Circle one/fill in blank.*
        a.   No
        b.   Yes. If yes, on the average, about how many cigarettes a day
             do you smoke? (1 pack = 20 cigarettes)
             1.   Number of cigarettes _____
             2.   Don't know/not sure

11.   Do you currently use any smokeless tobacco products such as
        chewing tobacco or snuff? *Circle one.*
        a.   Yes, chewing tobacco
        b.   Yes, snuff
        c.   Yes, both
        d.   No, neither
        e.   Don't know/not sure

        11A. Are you exposed to secondhand smoke?
              1.   No
              2.   Yes, at home
              3.   Yes, at work
              4.   Yes, at home and work
              5.   Yes, at public facilities

12.   Have the children in your house received immunizations (shots)
        against childhood diseases? *Circle one.*
        a.   No
        b.   Yes, all immunizations
        c.   Some, not all
        d.   Does not apply

13.   About how much do you weigh without shoes? *Circle one/fill in blank.*
        a.   ————— (pounds)
        b.   Don't know/not sure

14.   About how tall are you without shoes? *Circle one/fill in blank.*
        a.   ————— ft.   ————— inches
        b.   Don't know/not sure

15.   Are you now trying to lose weight? *Circle one.*
        a.   Yes
        b.   No
        c.   Don't know/not sure

16.   Are you concerned about unsupervised youth in your community?
        a.   Yes
        b.   No
        c.   Don't know/not sure

PART IV. QUESTIONS PERTAINING TO YOUR HEALTH

1.   Would you say that in general your health is: (*Circle one*)
        a.   Excellent
        b.   Very good
        c.   Good
        d.   Fair
        e.   Poor
        f.   Don't know/not sure

2.   Thinking about your physical health, which includes physical
        illness and injury, for how many days during the past 30 days was
        your physical health <u>not good</u>? *Circle one/fill in blank.*
        a.   ————— days
        b.   None
        c.   Don't know/not sure

3.   Thinking about your mental health, which includes stress, depres-
        sion, and problems with emotions, for how many days during the
        past 30 days was your mental health <u>not good</u>? *Circle one/fill in
        blank.*
        a.   ————— days
        b.   None
        c.   Don't know/not sure

4.   During the past 30 days, for about how many days did poor
        physical or mental health keep you from doing your usual activi-
        ties, such as self-care, work, or recreation? *Circle one/fill in blank.*
        a.   _____ days
        b.   None
        c.   Don't know, not sure

5.   During the last 3 months, did you visit or call a health care
        professional because of any kind of injury or accident? *Circle one.*
        a.   Yes
        b.   No

6.   During the last 3 months, did you miss more than half a day from
        school, work, household or usual activities because of an injury or
        accident? *Circle one.*
        a.   Yes
        b.   No

Women's Health   (to be filled out by only women respondents)

7.   A mammogram is an x-ray of each breast to look for breast cancer.
        Have you ever had a mammogram? *Circle one.*
        a.   Yes (Go to question 8)
        b.   No (Go to part V, question 1)
        c.   Don't know/not sure

If you have ever had a mammogram:
8.   How long has it been since the last mammogram? *Circle one.*
                a.   Within the past year (1 to 12 months ago)
                b.   Within the past 2 years (1 to 2 years ago)
                c.   Within the past 3 years (2 to 3 years ago)
                d.   Within the past 5 years (3 to 5 years ago)
                e.   5 or more years ago

PART V. DEMOGRAPHIC INFORMATION

1.   What is your race? *Circle one.*
        a.   White
        b.   Black
        c.   American Indian, Alaska Native
        d.   Asian, Pacific Islander
        e.   Spanish, Hispanic
        f.   Other

2.   What is your current marital status? *Circle one.*
   a.   Married
   b.   Divorced
   c.   Widowed
   d.   Separated
   e.   Never been married
   f.   Member of an unmarried couple

3.   What is the highest grade or year of school you completed?
       Circle one.
   a.   Never attended school, or kindergarten only
   b.   Grades 1 through 8 (elementary)
   c.   Grades 9 through 11 (some high school)
   d.   Grade 12 or GED certificate (high school graduate)
   e.   College, 1 year to 3 years (some college or technical school)
   f.   College, 4 years or more (college graduate)

4.   What is your current employment status? *Circle one.*
   a.   Employed for wages (Go to question 5)
   b.   Self-employed (Go to question 5)
   c.   Out of work for more than 1 year (Go to question 6)
   d.   Out of work for less than 1 year (Go to Question 6)
   e.   Homemaker (Go to question 6)
   f.   Student (Go to question 6)
   g.   Retired (Go to question 6)
   h.   Unable to work (Go to question 6)

5.   If you are currently employed, what is your current occupation?
       Circle one.
   a.   Farm work
   b.   Agricultural services
   c.   Construction
   d.   Manufacturing
   e.   Transportation, public utilities
   f.   Wholesale trade
   g.   Retail trade
   h.   Finance, insurance, real estate
   i.   Services
   j.   Federal civilian government
   k.   Federal military
   l.   State or local government
   m.   Education
   n.   Health services
   o.   Other (please specify _____)

6. How long have you lived in Howard County? *Circle one.*
    a. Less than a year
    b. 1-4 years
    c. 5-9 years
    d. 10-19 years
    e. 20 years plus

7. Where do you live? *Circle one.*
    a. In town
    b. On a farm with annual sales of agricultural products of $1,000 or more
    c. Neither in town nor on a farm (as defined in b)

8. Who has lived in your home (at least 50% of the time) in the last 12 months?

	Age	Sex (M = Male, F = Female)
You	____	____
Person 2	____	____
Person 3	____	____
Person 4	____	____
Person 5	____	____
Person 6	____	____
Person 7	____	____
Person 8	____	____
Person 9	____	____
Person 10	____	____

9. What is your annual household income? *Circle one.*
    a. Less than $10,000
    b. $10,000 to less than $15,000
    c. $15,000 to less than $20,000
    d. $20,000 to less than $25,000
    e. $25,000 to less than $35,000
    f. $35,000 to less than $50,000
    g. $50,000 to less than $75,000
    h. Over $75,000
    i. Don't know/not sure

Thank you for completing this survey.